World Bank Comparative Studies
THE POLITICAL ECONOMY OF POVERTY, EQUITY, AND GROWTH
Research Paper Number 3

World Bank Discussion Papers

Education and Its Relation to Economic Growth, Poverty, and Income Distribution

Past Evidence and Further Analysis

Jandhyala B. G. Tilak

The World Bank
Washington, D.C.

Copyright © 1989
The World Bank
1818 H Street, N.W.
Washington, D.C. 20433, U.S.A.

All rights reserved
Manufactured in the United States of America
First printing February 1989

Discussion Papers are not formal publications of the World Bank. They present preliminary and unpolished results of country analysis or research that is circulated to encourage discussion and comment; citation and the use of such a paper should take account of its provisional character. The findings, interpretations, and conclusions expressed in this paper are entirely those of the author(s) and should not be attributed in any manner to the World Bank, to its affiliated organizations, or to members of its Board of Executive Directors or the countries they represent. Any maps that accompany the text have been prepared solely for the convenience of readers; the designations and presentation of material in them do not imply the expression of any opinion whatsoever on the part of the World Bank, its affiliates, or its Board or member countries concerning the legal status of any country, territory, city, or area or of the authorities thereof or concerning the delimitation of its boundaries or its national affiliation.

Because of the informality and to present the results of research with the least possible delay, the typescript has not been prepared in accordance with the procedures appropriate to formal printed texts, and the World Bank accepts no responsibility for errors.

The material in this publication is copyrighted. Requests for permission to reproduce portions of it should be sent to Director, Publications Department at the address shown in the copyright notice above. The World Bank encourages dissemination of its work and will normally give permission promptly and, when the reproduction is for noncommercial purposes, without asking a fee. Permission to photocopy portions for classroom use is not required, though notification of such use having been made will be appreciated.

The complete backlist of publications from the World Bank is shown in the annual *Index of Publications,* which contains an alphabetical title list and indexes of subjects, authors, and countries and regions; it is of value principally to libraries and institutional purchasers. The latest edition of each of these is available free of charge from Publications Sales Unit, Department F, The World Bank, 1818 H Street, N.W., Washington, D.C. 20433, U.S.A., or from Publications, The World Bank, 66, avenue d'Iéna, 75116 Paris, France.

Jandhyala B. G. Tilak, an economist, is a consultant to the Human Resources Division of the World Bank's Latin America and the Caribbean Regional Office.

Library of Congress Cataloging-in-Publication Data

```
Tilak, Jandhyala B. G.
   Education and its relation to economic growth, poverty, and income
 distribution : past evidence and further analysis / Jandhyala B.G.
 Tilak.
       p.   cm. -- (The Political economy of poverty, equity, and
 growth ; research paper no. 3)  (World Bank discussion papers ; 46)
     Bibliography: p.
     ISBN 0-8213-1181-6
     1. Education--Economic aspects.  2. Economic development--Effect
 of education on.  3. Income distribution.  I. Title.  II. Series.
 III. Series: World Bank comparative studies.  Political economy of
 poverty, equity, and growth ; research paper no. 3.
 HC79.E47T55  1989
 338.9--dc19                                                 89-5279
                                                                 CIP
```

ABSTRACT

An education explosion has taken place in all countries of the world during the last few decades. How does this relate to economic growth, poverty and income distribution? This paper presents an extensive survey of empirical research evidence on this issue, and makes a fresh empirical analysis of the role of education in income distribution, with a slightly improved specification and using the latest available data on alternative measures of income distribution, viz., the Gini coefficient of income inequality, income shares of various population groups by income classes, and poverty ratios. The analysis reconfirms some of the well established theses on the role of education in improving income distribution, partly questions some of the doubts expressed by critics, indicates that with significant increases in educational levels of the population through out the world, the threshold level of education for it to significantly contribute to income distribution could change from primary to secondary education, and on the whole, reasserts that education is an important policy instrument that can be looked upon with hope towards improving income inequalities.

The structure of the paper is as follows: Part I presents a glimpse of the education explosions, the world has experienced; Part II surveys the fastly growing research on the relationship between education and economic growth, poverty and income distribution, including the perverse effects of public subsidization of higher education; Part III examines afresh a few selective dimensions relating to the role of education in improving poverty and income distribution with the latest data; and Part IV presents a short summary of the work, along with a few concluding observations.

FOREWORD

This is one in the series of research publications of the World Bank Comparative Study on the Political Economy of Poverty, Equity and Growth.

The entire project, which focuses on twenty one countries, has several purposes. For each country a monograph is being written which outlines the major forces underlying the country's performance with regard to poverty, equity and growth.

In addition, a series of special studies have been prepared focussing on themes such as education, nutrition, health, food subsidies, the military, and labor force participation and their relationship with poverty, equity and growth. These special studies do not necessarily confine to the twenty one countries.

This research paper presents an extensive survey of empirical research evidence on the role of education in economic growth, poverty and income distribution. The author also makes a fresh analysis of more recent cross nation data on education and income distribution. The analysis that uses lagged variables on education, reconfirms some of the well established theses on the role of education in improving income distribution. It also indicates that with significant improvements in educational levels of the population throughout the world, the threshold level of education for it to significantly contribute to income distribution could change from primary to secondary education. The author also questions some of the doubts expressed by critics in this context and reasserts that, on the whole, education is an important policy instrument that can be looked upon with hope towards improving income inequities.

Deepak Lal
Hla Myint
George Psacharopoulos
Project Directors

Acknowledgements

The author acknowledges with gratitude the incisive comments made by George Psacharopoulos, who has patiently read the earlier drafts and suggested several improvements at various stages. The author also benefited from the comments by Rati Ram. The usual caveats follow.

CONTENTS

I	Education Explosion	1
II	Earlier Research	10
	2.1 Education and Economic Growth	10
	2.2 Education and Agricultural Productivity	23
	2.3 Education and Income Distribution	28
	2.4 Public Subsidization of Education and Equity	44
	2.5 A Summary of Earlier Evidence	59
III	New Evidence	63
	3.1 The Data	63
	3.2 Education and Poverty	64
	3.3 Education and Income Distribution	73
	3.4 Public Subsidization of Higher Education and Income Inequality	84
	3.5 A Brief Summary	87
IV	Concluding Observations	89
	References	94
	Appendix	110

LIST OF TABLES

Table 1	Growth in Adult Literacy	4
Table 2	Growth in Enrollments	5
Table 3	Growth in Enrollment Ratios	6
Table 4	Growth in Public Expenditure on Education	7
Table 5	Contribution of Education to Economic Growth by Region	14
Table 6	Returns to Investment in Education	20
Table 7	Farmer Education and Farm Productivity	26
Table 8	Effect of Education on Income Distribution: Evidence from Cross-Country Studies	35
Table 9	Incidence of Unemployment among Households with Different Levels of Income in Greater Bombay, India (1971)	43
Table 10	Public Subsidization of Education	46
Table 11	Distribution of Students in Higher Education, by Income	48
Table 12	Distribution of Resources for Education	49
Table 13	Distribution of Education Subsidies by Income Group	55
Table 14	Schooling and Poverty	65
Table 15	Explaining Poverty: I	69
Table 16	Explaining Poverty: II	72
Table 17	Explaining Income Shares: I	76
Table 18	Explaining Income Shares: II	78
Table 19	Explaining the Income Share of the Bottom 40% Population	80
Table 20	Explaining the Income Share of the Middle 40% Population	81

Table 21 Explaining the Income Share of the Top 20% Population   83

Table 22 Higher Education Subsidy and Income Inequality:
         Regression Estimates for Gini   86

Appendix Tables

Table A.1 Means and Standard Deviations of the Variables   110

Table A.2 Coefficients of Correlation among the Education
         Variables, 1984   111

Table A.3 Coefficients of Correlation between Current and
         Lagged Education Variables   112

List of Figures

Figure 1 Growth in Enrollments and Literacy   2

Figure 2 Distribution of Personal Income and Subsidies   57

I. Education Explosion

During the last three to four decades, the world has experienced an education explosion. In all countries of the world, one can find an unprecedented inflation in numbers. The world enrollments in all levels of education, from the primary to the tertiary, expanded from about 250 million in 1950 to 906 million in 1985. It increased by more than 3.5 times, rising at an annual rate of growth of about 7.5 percent. During this period, as much as one-third of the increase in the total population was absorbed in education institutions as student enrollments. More than half of the population of the age group 6-24 in the world are presently in schools and colleges. Between 1960 and 1985, a period for which more detailed data are available, adult literates in the world doubled from 1,134 million to 2,314 million, increasing at an annual rate of growth of 3.8 percent. In 1985, of the estimated world population of 3,200 million, nearly three-fourths are literate. During the same period, public expenditure on education increased by about 13 times from $53.8 thousand

FIGURE 1

GROWTH IN ENROLLMENTS AND ADULT LITERACY
(1960-1985)

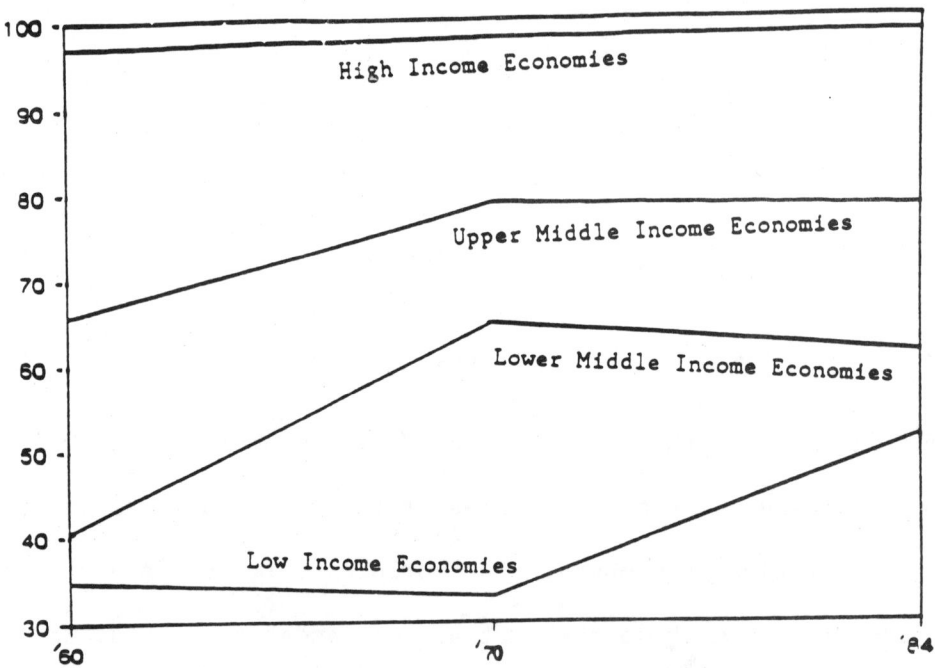

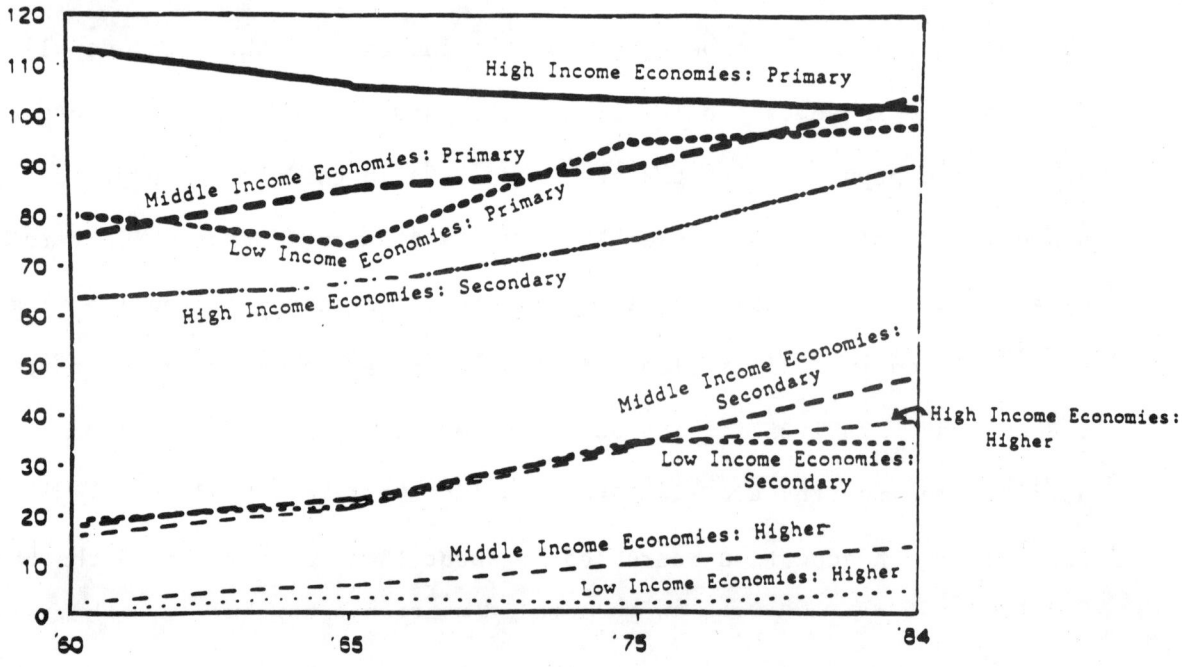

Source: Based on Tilak (1988b).

million to $689.6 thousand million (in current prices). As a percentage of world national product, which takes care of price increase, the increase has been from 3.9 in 1960 to 5.8 in 1985. As Patel (1985, p.1314) comments, "it is difficult to imagine any comparable period in the world history when the education expansion was so rapid, the numbers involved so overwhelming."

The education explosion is truly global in nature. All countries of the world, developing and developed, experienced this, as can be seen in Figure 1. However, the share of the developing countries in the expansion of the world education system is quite high, as can be noted from Tables 1 through 4. Enrollments increased at an average annual rate of growth of 12 percent at primary, 37 percent at secondary and 43 percent at higher levels in developing countries, compared to -0.8 percent at primary, 2.9 percent at secondary, and 9.6 percent at higher education in the developed countries. The total enrollments as a proportion of the age-group population of 6-24 in all levels of education increased from 26.8 percent in 1960 to 56 percent in 1985. Adult literacy increased in the developing countries by 21 percentage points during the 25 year period. Primary enrollment ratio has increased by 25 percentage points during the same period. Public expenditure on education increased by 13.5 times in developing countries (in current prices) during 1960-85, compared to 9.9 times in the developed countries. This tremendous growth is of course to be seen against the relatively small bases at which these developing economies started. Nevertheless, they reflect significant achievements. The rates of growth are higher in developing countries not only than the present developed countries as we note in these tables, but also they are higher than the rates of growth of the developed countries at 'comparable'

Table 1

GROWTH IN ADULT LITERACY
(percent)

	1960	1985	Change
Low income economies	34.7	51.8	17.1
Middle income economies	52.6	69.2	16.6
Lower middle income economies	40.5	61.6	21.1
Upper middle income economies	65.8	78.6	12.8
Industrial Market economies	97.0	98.3	1.3
Developing countries	40.8	61.8	21.0
Developed countries	95.1	97.9	2.8
World Total	60.7	72.3	11.6

Source: Tilak (1988b),
UNESCO Statistical Yearbook(s), and
"The Current Literacy Situation in the World," Paris: UNESCO, 1987.

Table 2

GROWTH IN ENROLLMENTS
(millions)

	Developing Countries			Developed Countries			World Total		
	1960	1985	% Change per Year	1960	1985	% Change per Year	1960	1985	% Change per Year
Primary	118.9	474.5	2.0	124.5	104.6	-0.8	243.5	579.1	5.6
Secondary	18.2	184.3	36.5	50.7	87.7	2.9	68.9	271.9	11.8
Higher	2.1	24.7	43.1	9.1	30.9	9.6	11.2	55.7	15.9
Total	139.3	683.5	15.6	184.3	223.3	0.9	323.6	906.7	7.2

Source: UNESCO Statistical Yearbook(s).

Table 3

GROWTH IN ENROLLMENT RATIOS (%)

	Primary			Secondary			Higher		
	1960	1985	Change	1960	1985	Change	1960	1985	Change
Lower Income Countries	79.5	97.0	17.5	17.5	32.0	14.5	2.1	4.0	1.9
Middle Income Countries	77.5	104.0	26.5	16.6	47.0	30.4	3.5	13.0	9.5
Lower Middle Countries	68.2	103.0	34.8	10.5	40.0	29.5	2.6	12.0	9.4
Upper Middle Countries	87.7	105.0	17.3	23.2	56.0	32.8	4.4	15.0	10.6
Industrial Market Economies	113.0	102.0	-11.0	63.9	90.0	26.1	15.8	38.0	22.2
Developing Countries	72.8	97.8	25.0	15.1	37.7	22.6	2.0	6.4	4.4
Developed Countries	101.5	102.3	0.8	62.1	87.9	25.8	13.3	33.1	19.8
World Total	62.3	76.8	14.5	37.9	55.6	17.7	8.0	19.4	11.4

Source: Tilak (1988b), and
last 3 categories: UNESCO Statistical Yearbook(s).

Table 4

GROWTH IN PUBLIC EXPENDITURE ON EDUCATION

	% of GNP			per Inhabitant at current prices (US$)		
	1960	1985	Change	1960	1985	% Change per Year
Developing Countries	2.4	4.1	1.7	2	27	50.0
Developed Countries	4.2	6.2	2.0	52	515	35.6
World Total	3.9	5.8	1.9	18	147	28.7

Source: UNESCO Statistical Yearbook(s).

stages of development (see Patel 1985). In this sense, the unquenching thirst of the people of the newly independent countries for mastering the magic of enlightenment resulted in a rapid increase in education numbers of all kinds, creating what is called an "educational miracle in the Third World" (Patel 1985).[1]

All this growth in education in the world has had a significant impact on not only productivity and economic growth, but also on poverty and income inequalities. The relationship between education and economic development is not just one way. In the infant years of economics of education, much controversy prevailed on the 'chicken and egg' relationship between education and economic growth (Vaizey 1962). Education is both 'a flower and seed of economic development' (Harbison and Myers 1964). There is a good amount of literature on the effect of economic growth on the growth of education. However, we concentrate here on the other relationship only, i.e., the contribution of education to economic development. This is not to undermine the importance of influence of economic conditions on the growth of education.

The present paper makes a modest attempt at documenting some of the important research on this problem, viz., the contribution of education to economic growth, poverty and income distribution, that has during the last three decades grown into a 'colossus,' enriching all branches of economic analysis: micro economics, labor economics, capital theory, growth theory, agricultural economics and, above all, income distribution theories (Sahota 1978, p.11). The present paper does not claim to be

---

[1] See also Horn and Arriagada (1986) for an account of three decades of progress in education in the world, and Benavot and Riddle (1988) for a discussion on expansion of primary education in a longer historical context.

exhaustive. Rather it is not possible in a study of this size.[2] The survey in Part II of this paper is divided into three sections: Section 2.1 reviews quickly the abundant research on education and economic growth, followed by a brief review of research on effects of education on agricultural development in Section 2.2. Section 2.3 is devoted to a survey of empirical research evidence on the relationship between education and income distribution. Effects of public subsidization on income distribution are reviewed in Section 2.4. Section 2.5 presents a short summary of the survey. In Part III we attempt at an another empirical exercise with more recent data and slightly more improved specification. However, this exercise is confined to an analysis of relationship between education, poverty and income distribution. Further, a few selective aspects of the problem are only investigated. After a brief discussion on data in Section 3.1, Section 3.2 analyzes the effect of education on poverty, which is relatively less extensively studied, compared to examination of relative income inequality and education relationships, which we examine in Section 3.3, and Section 3.4 is concerned with public subsidization of higher education and income inequality. The paper ends with a brief summary and a few concluding observations (Part IV).

---

[2] Major surveys of the literature, though not very recent include Mincer (1970), Blaug (1976), and Rosen (1976).

II. Earlier Research

2.1 Education and Economic Growth

The role of education in development has been recognized ever since the days of Plato. Education, Plato believed, is indispensable to the economic health of a good society, for education makes citizens 'reasonable men'. Since education has high economic value, Plato argued that a considerable part of the community's wealth must be invested in education. Major contribution to the discussion on education-economic growth relationship was made first by Adam Smith followed by a long honorable tradition of classical and neo-classical economists until Alfred Marshall in the 20th century who emphasized that "the most valuable of all capital is that invested in human beings". However in the modern period, the inability of the conventional theories of economic growth to explain more than a half of growth with the help of factors like labor and capital, led to the rediscovery of the role of human capital in economic growth in the 1950s. The rediscovery created what is later aptly described as the "human investment revolution in economic thought" (Bowman 1966). Schultz's (1961a and 1961b) pioneering works that led to this revolution and established that education is not merely a consumption activity, but is an investment that leads to the formation of human capital comparable to physical capital, were followed by a significant and rapid growth in research on the relationship between education and economic development.

Education transforms the raw human beings into productive 'human capital' by inculcating the skills required by both the traditional sector and the modern sector of the economy,[3] and makes the individuals more productive not only in the market place but also in the household. Education, including both technical training and general education, contributes to economic growth through its ability to increase the productivity of the population or the labor force in particular, which leads to increase in individuals' earnings. The core of the human capital theory lies in this thesis that education increases productivity of the labor force leading to increase in economic growth.

In the beginning, the unexplained proportion of economic growth, <u>viz</u>., the "residual," was attributed to "technical progress" (Solow 1957; and Svennilson 1964). Later works (e.g., Denison 1962; and Griliches and Jorgenson 1966) clearly established that this residual was not "a coefficient of ignorance," as some critics (Balogh 1963;) argued, but human capital, particularly education forms a significant proportion of this residual. With Griliches' (1964, and 1970) works, it was made clear that education could enter as an important variable (input) in the production function analysis.

Starting from Aukrust (1959), who found the residual that is attributable to human factor, to be 1.81 percent of the growth in the Norwegian economy, several scholars worked on the 'residual' method. Pioneering works were carried out in the United States. Denison (1962) estimated that 23 percent of the growth rate in per capita (employed) income between 1909-29 in the United States could be due to education, and the corresponding figure was as high as 42 percent during 1929-57.

---

[3] See Chiswick (1982) for more details.

According to his later works (Denison 1974), it was found that 21 percent of the growth during 1948-73 was due to increased levels of education of the labor force. Kendrick (1977; see also 1981) and Jorgenson (1984) also estimated that education accounted for 15-25 percent of growth in GNP per capita in the US during 1948-76. Further, Haveman and Wolfe (1984) found that the impact of education might be increasing.

The effect of education cannot be constant all the time. It varied in the United States over the years (Walters and Rubinson 1983). Analyzing the impact of education on the national output during 1890 to 1969, Walters and Rubinson found that primary and secondary schooling had significant and positive 10-year lagged effects on national output during the pre-Depression period, and secondary education had a strong 20-year lagged effect in the post-Depression period.

Denison's and Schultz's famous growth accounting equations were replicated by many scholars. In a recent survey, Psacharopoulos (1984, p.337; also in 1973, p.116) reports first generation estimates of the contribution of education to economic growth using either of the two equations, for 29 countries. According to these estimates, the contribution of education to economic growth expressed as a percentage of the observed rate of economic growth "explained" by education ranged between 0.8 percent in Mexico and 25 percent in Canada, the simple average being 8.7 percent.[4] Psacharopoulos (1973, p.117) further analyzed the same to show that the contribution of education declines by increasing

---

[4] Psacharopoulos (1984, pp.340-41; see also Selowsky 1969), however, argues that all these estimates were underestimates, as the education maintenance component of growth in labor force was not taken into account, and this caused a downward bias ranging between 38 percent in the United States to 90 percent in India in estimates of the contribution of education.

levels of per capita income as shown in Table 5. In Africa it was about 17.2 percent, compared to 11.1 percent in Asia and 8.6 percent in North America and Europe.[5]

A substantial proportion of income differences among countries could also be explained with the help of human capital models. Krueger (1968) found that education, age and sectoral distribution of population explained more than half of the differences in income levels between the United States and a group of 28 countries. Education alone could explain one-quarter to one-third in this context. In some countries as high as 63 percent of the gap in per capita income was attributed to human capital stocks. Even the countries which had same factor endowments as the US could not attain the level of United States per capita income due to 'educational gap'. Kothari (1970) also presented a similar analysis on the income differences between a few countries, particularly India and United Kingdom.

Various approaches were adopted in the context of international comparisons; but most studies yielded similar results. In one of the earliest major cross-country studies, Bowman and Anderson (1963) analyzed the relationship between literacy and economic development. They found that literacy contributed significantly to economic growth. A 40 percent adult literacy rate was a necessary, but not a sufficient, condition for an economy to reach a GNP per capita level of US$200 (in 1950), and it was only when literacy rate exceeds 80 percent, that GNP per capita could cross $500. They also found from the evidence of 77 countries that primary

---

5/ However, in North America, the rate of return is the highest, 20 percent.

Table 5

THE CONTRIBUTION OF EDUCATION TO ECONOMIC GROWTH BY REGION

Region		Percentage of growth rate explained by education
Africa	(3)	17.2
Asia	(4)	11.1
Latin America	(9)	5.1
North America & Europe	(13)	8.6
North America	(2)	20.0
Europe	(11)	6.5
All countries	(29)	8.7

Note: Figures are simple country averages within regions and mostly refer to the economic growth rate in the 1950s and 1960s.
Figures in ( ) refer to the number of countries in each category.

Source: Based on Psacharopoulos (1984, p.337).

enrollments in 1930s had a substantial explanatory power for income levels 20 years later, i.e., in 1955 (see also Bowman 1980).

Peasle (1965; and 1967) correlated primary school enrollments and GNP per capita in 34 richest countries of the world since 1850 and found that no country has ever achieved significant economic growth within the last 100 years without first attaining an enrollment ratio of 10 percent at primary level, which in other words, was absolutely essential for any economy to 'take off'.

Adam Curle (1964) correlated educational indicators in the mid-1950s and per capita income in 1954-59 in 50 countries, and found a correlation coefficient of 0.53 between GNP per capita and percentage proportion of GNP invested in education, and 0.64 between GNP per capita and post-primary enrollments. Similarly Bennett (1967) found in a study on 69 countries, high correlation between GNP per capita and secondary vocational education and low correlation between GNP per capita and general secondary education.[6]

McClelland (1966) found significant positive correlation between secondary school enrollments in 1930 in 21 developed countries and the rate of economic growth between 1929 an 1950. In another cross-country study of 75 countries, Harbison and Myers (1964) found high correlation between per capita GNP and secondary and higher educational levels.

Recent works that used econometric methods also produced similar conclusions on the role of literacy and education. Razin (1977) found from cross-country data on 11 developed countries for the period 1953-65, a

---

[6] Bennett (1967) also found that enrollments in vocational education, as a ratio of general secondary education, increased in countries upto a GNP per head level of $500, and then declines with increase in income levels.

significant effect of education on economic growth. Hicks (1980) analyzed the relationship between literacy and economic growth in 83 countries for the period 1960-77 and found that an average increase in the literacy rate by 20 percentage points is associated with 0.5 percent higher growth rate. Hicks further noted that only those economies are rapidly growing that had above average levels of performance in literacy and life expectancy.

Stronger relationship was found between literacy and economic development by Wheeler (1980). He found from his simultaneous equations which allow two-way relationships on differences in economic growth and literacy in 88 countries, for the period 1960-63 and 1970-73 and pooled data for the entire period, that an increase in literacy from 20 percent to 30 percent resulted in an increase in real GDP by 8 percent to 16 percent. In the case of African countries, the effect of literacy was found to be much higher.

Marris (1982) extending the work of Wheeler made estimates for 37 middle-income and 29 low-income countries for 1965-73 and 1973-78, and not only reaffirmed the importance of education in economic growth, but also found a relatively weak role of investment in physical capital, such as in construction and in fixed tangible assets, in economic growth unless supported by education. He found that inter-country differences in primary education enrollment ratios significantly affect the rate of growth of per capita incomes. According to Marris, a one percentage point difference in primary enrollment ratio was associated with 0.035 percentage points in inter-country differences in per capita income growth rates. Further, defining benefits as the gain in per capita incomes and costs as the income loss associated with the use of resources in the particular activity, Marris estimated benefit-cost ratios for primary education enrollment to be

7.4 percent in 1965-73 and 6.4 percent in 1973-79 in middle-income countries, and 7.1 percent and 3.4 percent in low-income countries in the respective periods. By comparison, the benefit-cost ratios for physical investment were very low, less than or equal to 1.0 percent.

Once it was established that education, in general, is positively and significantly related to economic growth, researchers were interested in inquiring which level of education contributes most to economic growth. Quite a few studies are available on this question as well. Lee and Psacharopoulos (1979) found strong correlation between educational indicators in 1960 and economic indicators in 1970 in 114 countries. The correlation is higher in the case of literacy and primary education, and in the case of low income countries, compared to middle and high income countries.

In another study, Meyer et al (1979) also found significant positive effects of primary and secondary education in 1950-65 and 1965-70 respectively, while higher education had always a negative and statistically insignificant effect. Meyer et al., also found that the effect of secondary education is higher than that of primary education.

In a recent work, Benavot (1985) also studied the impact of various levels of education on GNP per capita on 50-110 developed and developing countries, depending upon the availability of data. The panel regression results indicated that primary education has a significant and positive effect on economic growth during all periods (1930 to 1980) both in developed and developing countries. Secondary education has a strong negative effect in less developed countries and weak and positive effect in the developed countries during 1930-50, and had a positive effect both in developed and developing countries during 1955-70, and during 1965-80 the effect of secondary education was weakened; and tertiary education had little to do with economic development.

Thus, it is important to note that the role of education as an instrument of economic growth varies over time. Education may yield substantial rewards at some stages of development, while at other stages, the impact may be negligible. There may be not only a threshold level of literacy/education for it to influence economic development, but also a threshold level of economic development for literacy/education to grow, and for it to influence significantly the education development. For example, literacy may be a pre-requisite for sustained growth, but demand for literacy and schooling itself may depend upon the level of socio-economic development (see e.g., AERC 1971; Shortlidge 1973; and Wolfe and Behrman 1984).[7] As a result, in sum, the influence of education on economic development varies by the stage of development of the economy. This has been repeatedly highlighted in the research on education and economic growth.

Cross-section comparisons, without introducing a time lag, also led Tilak (1986) to arrive at more or less similar conclusions. Tilak classified the 75 countries into four categories, *viz*., very poor, poor, rich and very rich countries. Tilak finds that while on the whole, there is a significant positive relationship between education development and economic growth of the nations, the relationship is strong in the very poor countries, and rich countries, but is not significant in very rich countries and poor countries. Further, while in very poor countries, primary and secondary education have relatively more significant role in

---

[7] As stated earlier, this aspect is kept outside the scope of the present paper.

economic development, in the rich countries secondary and higher education have significant impact, and primary education is found to be statistically not significantly related.

Estimates of Denison-type equations for several countries (see Psacharopoulos 1973, p.119) also revealed that the contribution of primary education is much higher than that of higher education and that of secondary education. Only in a few cases, the contribution of secondary education exceeds the contribution of primary education.

Another area of evidence, bulging in quantity, relates to rates of return to education. From Strumilin (1929), the first attempt on cost benefits analysis in education, and Becker (1960), the first more systematic attempt after the beginning of the human investment revolution, to date, we have a large number of studies on rates of return to education. In a recent update, Psacharopoulos (1985) summarized estimates relating to about 60 countries, covering almost all parts of the world, developed and developing countries in Asia, Africa, Australia, Europe, North and South America, and they are presented in in summary form in Table 6.

The large evidence can be briefly summarized as follows:

o The social returns to education in developing countries are at least as high as any reasonable measure of the opportunity cost of capital or social discount rate. In other words, investment in human capital in general, and in education in particular, may be more conducive to economic growth than investment in physical capital.

o Rates of return are highest in primary education, followed by secondary and then university levels. For primary education, unit costs are small relative to the extra lifetime income or

Table 6

RETURNS TO INVESTMENT IN EDUCATION
(percent)

Country Group	Social Rate of Return			Private Rate of Return		
	Primary	Secondary	Higher	Primary	Secondary	Higher
Africa	26	17	13	45	26	32
Asia	27	15	13	31	15	18
Latin America	26	18	16	32	23	23
Intermediate Countries*	13	10	8	17	13	13
Industrial Market Economies	-	11	9	-	12	12

Note: - Not available because of lack of control group of illiterates.

* Refers to South European and Middle East countries.
Figures are averages for fifty-eight countries and mainly refer to the late 1970s.

Source: Psacharopoulos (1985, p.586).

productivity associated with literacy. For university education, the opposite is true.

o   The same diminishing returns apply across countries: the more developed the country, the lower the returns to education at all levels. The high returns to education in low-income countries must be attributed to their relative scarcity of human capital.

o   Private returns are higher than social returns at all levels--a result of the huge public subsidization of education in most countries. The discrepancy between private and social returns is greatest at higher education--which raises issues of equity as well as of how educational expansion should be financed.

Thus, there is an overwhelming evidence in support of the view that education is a productive investment that pays.

A few historical studies, however, produced different results. Expansion of education was found to be having little effect on economic output in the 19th century Germany (Lundgreen 1976). In Mexico, literacy had only a slightly positive effect on agricultural output in the 19th century (Fuller et al 1984). It is also cited that 18th century entrepreneurial innovators and inventors in Britain did not have the benefit of any systematic education (Ashby 1961). Historically one notices that, in the industrialized countries significant growth of formal education largely followed rather than preceded economic growth, while in the present developing countries economic growth follows education expansion (Levin et al 1982).

However, historical narrative evidences do not exactly corroborate to this view. Literacy was widely spread in the developed countries even at the beginning of the 19th century. By 1800, literacy had been acquired by the vast majority of males and about one-third of adult females in the countries of North America and north-western Europe. It suggests that "a substantial literacy base was necessary, if not a sufficient prerequisite for the massive economic transformation that occurred in the northern hemisphere during the eighteenth and nineteenth centuries" (Foster 1987, p.93). Similarly the rapid economic development in Japan was attributed to the development of human capital at the very initial stages (Emi 1968); so is the case of Soviet Russia (Komarov 1968), Taiwan (see Singer 1983), Israel and many other countries of the world (Easterlin 1961 and 1981).

A few more studies did of course find either weak or lack of relationship between education and economic growth. For example, Walters (1981) concluded that the economic growth rates between 1960-70 were least influenced by primary and secondary enrollment ratios in 1950, and by growth rates in primary and secondary enrollments during 1950-60, even though she found high correlation between primary enrollment in 1950 and log GNP per capita in 1960 and in 1970. An East African case study (Rado and Jolly 1965) also found no consistent relationship between economic development and secondary and higher education. Kanamori (1972) found that education accounts hardly one percent of the growth in Japan during 1955-68. [8]

There are also a few theories to argue that the productivity role of education is limited; education serves only a credential mechanism and a

---

[8]/ However, Kanamori (1972, p.160) himself called for a re-examination of the data and the methodology.

screening apparatus (Arrow 1973; and Spence 1973). Criticism was also levelled on the marginal productivity hypothesis of taking wages as reflective of productivity (e.g., Bhaduri 1978). But these theories lack strong empirical support. The screening role of education is found to be confined, if at all, to short periods, confining to the initial stages of employment. Quantitative evidence on the whole is still overwhelmingly in support of the human capital theory, a basic tenet of which is that education contributes positively to economic growth.[9] Attacks based on marginal productivity hypothesis also did not stand valid. That education contributes to growth in output was clearly reaffirmed further by studies that considered not monetary benefits, but physical (real) output benefits, particularly in agriculture. Let us briefly look at this.

2.2 Education and Agricultural Productivity

Several physical effects of education and agricultural development can be identified and quantified. Effects of education on the productivity of workers include (a) innovative effects such as ability to decode new information, know what, why, where and how; ability to estimate costs and benefits of alternatives, and ability to establish quicker access to newly available economically useful information; (b) allocative effects such as ability to choose optimum combinations of crops and agricultural practices in least number of trials, and ability to choose optimum time for marketing, transportation etc.; (c) worker effects such as ability to perform agricultural operations more efficiently in the economic sense; and (d) externalities (see Welch 1970; and also Schultz 1975). Cross-country

---

[9] See Blaug (1976) for a critique of the screening models and other attacks on human capital theory.

studies (e.g., Hayami and Ruttan 1970), and several micro studies (e.g., Griliches 1964; and Welch 1970) found a significant relationship between education and farm output. Hayami and Ruttan (1970, p.906) found that differences in educational levels explain one-quarter to one-half of the differences in agricultural labor productivity between the United States on the one hand, and Colombia, Egypt, India and Philippines on the other. Surveying evidence from 31 countries, Lockheed et al (1980)[10] concluded that on average education of four years of primary schooling of farmers would enhance the farm output by 8.7 percent. Some of this evidence is summarized in Table 7.

The other important details on the empirical evidence on the contribution of education to agricultural productivity can be noted as follows:

o Education significantly effects methods of production, use of modern inputs like fertilizers, seeds and machines, and selection of crops.

o Wages among landless agricultural laborers are also positively influenced by differences in their levels of education.

o There also exists a threshold level of education for its impact to be significant and while this level varies for different regions marginally and for different purposes, mostly it is secondary level of education of about 10 years of schooling.

o This threshold level of education is relevant not only for farm efficiency, but also for other activities like

---

10/ See also Jamison and Lau (1982).

utilization of credit facilities, adoption of family planning methods, etc.

o   As the economy develops, and technological developments take place, this threshold level goes up. For example in India, elementary education was the threshold level during the 1960s, while it was secondary level during the 1970s.

o   Socio-cultural factors and the caste system substantially influence the impact of education on agriculture productivity and other variations.

If we divide the research into two categories for a critical survey, viz., impact of education on agricultural productivity in high technology and better environmental conditions, and impact of education on agricultural productivity in low technology and poorer environmental conditions, we note that the impact is higher in the latter case than in high technology conditions. It is quite possible that in the areas of farming under better technological environment, the impact of education could be much smaller than estimated in aggregate situations.

Whether it is traditional farming, or farming based on intermediate technology or fully improved or advanced technology and/or fully irrigation based farming, the role of education is very important; but educational requirements of course vary by the type/state of farming. Simple numeracy may be adequate for traditional farming, numeracy and rudimentary literacy may be needed for farming with intermediate technology. Formal education of secondary and above that gives a basic knowledge of chemistry, biology, etc., besides mathematics would, be a basic requirement of farming based on improved technology or fully irrigation-based technology. The relationship between education and

Table 7

FARMER EDUCATION AND FARM PRODUCTIVITY

Country	Estimated % increase in Annual Farm Output due to 4 years of Primary Education than None.
With Complimentary Inputs*	
Brazil 1969-70	4.0 to 22.1
Colombia 1969	(-)0.8 to 24.4
Kenya 1971-72	6.9
Malaysia 1973	20.4
Nepal 1968-69	20.4
South Korea 1973	9.1
AVERAGE (unweighted)	13.2
Without Complimentary Inputs	
Brazil 1969-70	(-)3.6 to 10.8
Colombia 1969	12.4 to 12.5
Greece 1963	25.9
AVERAGE (unweighted)	8.1

Note: * improved seeds, irrigation, transport to market and so on.

Source: World Bank (1980, p.16).

technology is quite strong in the case of modern technology based agriculture. It is clear that numeracy is the basic pre-requisite having most significant effect on farm efficiency.

Looking at the same problem in another way, there exists a gap between best practice of farming and the current practice. Economic conditions, particularly the level of technology and agricultural prices significantly explain the best practice while the low levels of current practice could be attributed to, inter alia low levels of literacy and education. The path from current to the best practice is not a smooth one, as both go on changing in a dynamic sense. In this context literacy and general education, extension education and R&D (research and development) assume much importance. Their relative importance, however, is determined by the gap between the best and the current practices. One may intuitively argue that the smaller the gap, the larger would be the role of R&D and vice versa. But in all cases, literacy and basic education form minimum conditions.

In general, the role of research in agricultural development in any economy is quite significant. Advancement in research is a decisive factor in achieving increases in crop production throughout the world. In some countries the returns to investment in research are as high as 40 percent. Some other researchers estimated it to be 63 percent. The green revolution in India could be attributed largely to research and development activities besides, of course, to levels of literacy and education of the farmers. Of course, basic education prepared people for change.

Basically impact of education is not instantaneous; it is sequential. Production function approaches may not only assume that it has not only instantaneous effect, but also that it can be explained with the help of static data analysis. Perhaps the research in the area can be classified into two categories: one based on production function approaches and the other discrete approaches. Fortunately, both yield not altogether inconsistent results. The results on the whole reassert that education's effects on physical output are substantial, leading to improvement in productivity and economic growth.

Thus education-earnings relationship[11] is proved to be not superficial. Education contributes towards enhancement of productivity and thereby in wages and economic growth. The contribution of education to the other facets of development like improvements in health, fertility control, improvement in mortality and life expectancy etc., is well documented.[12] Similarly the consumption benefits of education and externalities of education are quite important. In fact it is argued that these benefits exceed the direct economic benefits of education.[13] However, we do not refer to these aspects here, and in the following section concentrate on the role of education in income distribution.

2.3 Education and Income Distribution

From the days of Adam Smith, education was believed to be a possible contributor to greater social and economic equality. Even prior to Adam Smith, we find references in the literature to the equity role of education. It was William Petty who first advocated equitable distribution

---

[11]/ See Blaug (1972) for an elaborate discussion on this aspect.

[12]/ See Cochrane et al (1980) for a survey on several of these aspects; Tilak (1987 and 1988a) for a survey of literature on education's effect on life expectancy and on infant mortality, respectively.

[13]/ See McMahon (1987a and 1987b) for an elaborate account of such benefits. See also Behrman (1987).

of education. Nehenia Green and James Stewart of the Mercantilist period also advocated mass education so as to increase agricultural productivity in particular and society's progress in general. Lord Palmerston favored the spread of literacy. The 18th and 19th century school reformers in the US like Horace Mann, Henry Barnard, James G Carter, Robert Dale Owen and George H Evans favored educational opportunities to be extended to the poorer groups. Horace Mann, a typical example of these reformers, viewed the school as an effective instrument to achieve justice and equality of opportunity and remove poverty. At least by the end of the 19th century the thesis was more clear. As early as in 1896 the role of education in reducing poverty was clearly recognized in Russia: "An increase of labor productivity is the only means to erase poverty in Russia and the best policy to achieve it is through the spread of education and knowledge" (Kahan 1963, pp.400-1).

Simon Kuznets (1955) predicted long back that income distribution in capitalist countries would become more equal as the labor force becomes more educated. Schultz (1963, p.65) had stated more clearly: "these changes in human capital [in the US] are a basic factor reducing the inequality in the personal distribution of income. This aspect has received the attention of the empirical researchers since the beginning of the 1970s. Education is argued to be vital to increase economic growth and to improve economic equality (Harbison 1973). Analyzing the problem in his numerous works, both from a positive point of view (Tinbergen 1977) and a normative point of view Tinbergen (1970 and 1980), concluded that human capital is one of the most important determinants of income inequality.

The relationship between education and income distribution is, however, somewhat complex, as education's effect on income inequality depends upon not only the way education is planned, developed and financed, but also it is contingent upon the socio economic factors, employment probabilities, wage structure, the fiscal base etc. For instance, changes in the pay offs to different levels of education also influence earnings distribution. If returns to higher education fall, relative to returns to investment in primary education, earnings distribution is likely to improve; on the other hand, if the opposite occurs, the increasing returns to higher education relative to returns to lower levels of education reflect a trend towards greater inequality. As Knight and Sabot (1983, p.1132) observed, "the change in educational composition of the labor force itself has an effect on inequality. Whether it raises or lowers inequality, <u>ceteris pari bus</u>, depends on the relative sizes of the different educational categories, their relative mean wages, and their relative wage dispersions."

However, the process of education effecting income distribution can be simply explained as follows: education creates a more skilled labor force. This will produce "a shift from low paid, unskilled employment to high paid, skilled employment. This shift, produces higher labor incomes, a reduction in skill differentials, and an increase in the share of wages in total output" (Ahluwalia 1976b, p.322). The increase in the number of more educated and skilled people will increase the ratio of such people and decrease the ratio of less educated people in the total labor force. In the labor market over supply of highly educated people results, given no change in demand, in lowering their wages and increase in the wages of those with less education, thus on the whole contributes to dimunition in income differences in the labor market. Thus expansion of education effects not only the wages of those who receive better education, but also of those who do not. In addition to that earnings distribution can be effected by education, as earnings and education are highly related, education may compensate for adverse socio economic background and open up better socio economic opportunities for the weaker sections of the society leading to faster mobility and higher wages. The financing pattern of education also influences income distribution. As education is largely state financed, the composition of relative shares of various income groups in state revenues, and the relative benefits received by various groups from education influences, if not exactly determines, income distribution. We examine some of these aspects in this and the following sections. We start with a few cross nation studies. Later we briefly refer to a few micro studies. Distribution of public subsidies to education forms the content of the next section.

The oft-quoted Adelman and Morris' (1973) cross-country study of 43 developing countries found that improvement in human resources, measured in terms of Harbison and Myers' (1964) index of human resource development which is a weighted average of enrollments at secondary and higher levels of education, was a significant determinant of income inequalities; it had a positive effect on the income shares of the bottom 40 percent and 60 percent population, and a negative effect on the shares of the top 20 percent and top 5 percent population. Accordingly they concluded that improvement of human resources was the only acceptable strategy for the decades ahead.

Chiwsick suggested that inequality in earnings should be positively related to inequality in investment in human capital, mean level of investment in human capital, average level of rate of return to human capital and inequality in rate of return to human capital. Regressing alternative earnings inequality measures on income per capita, rate of growth in incomes and educational inequality, Chiswick (1971) based on data on a small sample of 9 countries found that schooling inequality is directly related to earnings inequality, and hence improvement in schooling inequality could be an equalizer. Chiswick (1974) used a different variable for schooling, viz., interaction of rate of return to education and variance of schooling, in examining income inequalities in the US and Canada around 1960, and found this interaction variable to be having a strong positive effect on income inequalities. Chiswick (1974) finds that in US and a few other countries income inequality is greater the higher the rate of return to investment in education, and wider the variation in years of schooling.[14] Regional differences in level of income of male workers are related to differences in the distribution of schooling.

Chenery and Syrquin (1975) based on a sample of 50 countries came to a similar conclusion when adjusted enrollments in schools (primary and secondary levels) were used to explain income distribution. "High levels of education are associated with a shift of income away from top 20 percent, with a large proportion going to the bottom 40 percent than would otherwise be its share" (p.63).

Ahluwalia (1974) also found significant positive relationships between school enrollments and income equality. Using cross-country data on 66 countries, Ahluwalia fitted a regression equation. The estimated regression coefficients which show a significantly positive relationship between education and inequality, led him to conclude that education is positively related to equality in terms of income shares of the lowest and

---

[14] But Marin and Psacharopoulos (1976) pointed out that Chiswick's hypothesis requires independence between level of schooling and the rate of return to it. See also Fields (1980c).

middle groups, and more importantly that primary school enrollment ratio is more significant in explaining the income share of the bottom 40 percent population, while the secondary school enrollment rate is more significant in explaining that of the middle 40 percent. The secondary enrollment ratio and the income share of the top 20 percent are negatively related, suggesting that expansion of secondary education leads to redistribution of income away from top income quintile. Ahluwalia (1976b; also 1976a) used literacy variable also in the regression equation and provided more details. An increase in the literacy rate from 10 percent to 60 percent is associated with a 2.8 percentage point increase in the share of the lowest 40 percent population. Similarly, an increase in the secondary enrollment from 10 percent to 40 percent is associated with an increase of 4.6 percentage points in the income share of the middle 40 percent population. On the relative effects of literacy and secondary education, it was concluded that while literacy benefits the lower group, secondary schooling benefits the middle income group.

Tinbergen (1975) using the same data found a positive relationship between income inequality and the Lorenz coefficient of schooling in the labor force, and argued that "educational policies deserve to be programmed not only with a view to improving education in the widest sense, but also in order to influence income distribution. In most of our results... the equalizing consequences of extended education are reflected" (Tinbergen 1975, p.148). Further Tinbergen (1975, p.103) showed that economic growth does not automatically reduce income inequality. On the other hand, the race between technology and education is important. When education wins in this race, its impact on reduction in income inequality becomes significant.[15]

There are a few more important studies based on cross nation data, as documented in Table 8. Psacharopoulos (1977a; see also 1981) showed with the help of data on 49 countries, including 37 less developed countries, that educational distribution alone explains 23 percent of Gini coefficient of income inequality, and argued that a policy of more equal access to education (i.e., by flattening the educational pyramid) might have the desired impact of making income distribution more equal.

Another cross country study of 32 countries (Winegarden 1979) concludes that higher average levels of schooling exert an equalizing effect on income distribution. The mean level of educational achievement as well as the dispersion of education act as an equalizing influence on income disparities. Further, it was shown that inequalities in education play a large (larger than what the previous studies revealed) role in generating income disparities.

The effect of education on income inequality also varies by level of economic development. Leipziger and Lewis (1980)[16] found a negative and significant correlation coefficient between adult literacy rate and the Gini coefficient and a negative correlation between the Gini and the first level enrollment in the sample of 19 less developed countries with a per capita GNP level above $550 (in 1975). But in the case of another set of 19 countries whose GNP per capita was below $550 they found a positive and

---

[15]/ See also Schultz (1963, p.655) who hinted at the same, when he stated that as the investment in human capital expands rapidly relative to conventional physical capital, education becomes a significant factor in reducing income inequalities.

[16]/ See also Leipziger (1981).

Table 8

EFFECT OF EDUCATION ON INCOME DISTRIBUTION: EVIDENCE FROM CROSS-COUNTRY STUDIES

Source	Income Distribution Variable	Education Variable	Regression Coefficient	t-value	No. of Countries
Adelman and Morris (1973)	Income Shares of the	Improvement in Human Resources*			43
	Lowest 40% population		0.59	2.20	
	Lowest 60% population		0.70	2.60	
	Top 20% population		-2.50	2.60	
	Top 5% population		-7.20	1.80	
Chenery and Syrquin (1975)		Primary plus Secondary Enrollment Ratio			50
	Top 20% population		-0.223	3.08	
	Mid 40% population		0.155	3.31	
	Lowest 40% population		0.068	1.56	
Ahluwalia (1976b)	Income Shares of the	Secondary Enrollment Ratio			60
	Top 20% population		-0.219	4.32	
	Mid 40% population		-0.152	4.86	
	Bottom 40% population		0.066	2.53	
Psacharopoulos (1977a)	Gini Coefficient	Coefficient of Variation of enrollments	0.180	0.08++	49
Winegarden (1979)		Log. Education Level of the Adults			32
	Lowest 80% population	Mean	11.41	2.98	
		Variance	-18.68	2.18	
Ram (1984)		Mean Educational Level	1.605	1.67	28
	Lowest 80% population	Variance in Education	0.592	1.73	
Tilak (1986)		Enrollment Ratios			50
	Bottom 40% population	Primary	0.046	1.49	
		Secondary	0.073	3.42	
		Higher	0.011	2.75	
	Middle 40% population	Primary	0.109	0.96	
		Secondary	0.135	2.79	
		Higher	0.016	2.87	
	Top 20% population	Primary	-0.155	2.39	
		Secondary	-0.208	4.91	
		Higher	-0.027	3.13	
Leipziger and Lewis (1981)	Gini coefficient	Adult Literacy	-0.564+		19
	Gini coefficient	Primary Enrollment	-0.423+		19

Note: * Harbison-Myers' (1964) index of human resource development.
   + Coefficient of correlation (significant at 5% level).
   ++ Standard error.

however not significant correlation between the Gini coefficient and the literacy, and a negative correlation between the Gini coefficient and the first level enrollment.

In another cross-country study (Ram 1984) of a sample of 28 countries, out of which 26 were less developed, income shares of the bottom 40 and 80 percent population were alternatively regressed on a set of variables, including mean and variance of educational levels. In case where the income shares of the 40 percent population was the dependent variable, hardly any variable was significant; and in the other case, variance in educational levels turned out to be marginally significant. Further, while the variable on mean education level has an expected positive sign,[17] based on which, Ram concludes that "higher mean education appears to be an equalizer, and greater educational inequality is probably an income disequalizer" (p.420).

Rati Ram (1985)[18] in another study on basic needs found positive relationship between the income share of the lowest 40 percent population and elementary enrollment and adult literacy rates in the middle income less developed countries, but a negative relationship in the 9 low income less developed countries, indicating what we argued earlier that there is a threshold level of economic development for the education and income equality to be positively related. In another exercise on education expansion and schooling inequality, Ram (1987) observed that "expansion of

---

17/ The variable on variance in education also has a positive sign.

18/ Ram (1985) was, however, regressing adult literacy and enrollment on income levels and income shares, as he argues that the current levels of school enrollment may effect future and (not current) pattern of income distribution. See Ram (1981) where he presents significant OLS estimates when income inequality is regressed on educational inequality and <u>vice-versa</u>.

schooling may accentuate income inequality at early stages. At a later stage, however, the overall impact of educational expansion on income distribution is likely to be favorable."

Tilak (1986) also found with the help of data on 50 countries, a significant effect of education on the income shares of different groups of populations. Secondary enrollments have the most significant positive effect on the income shares of the bottom 40 percent and middle 40 percent population; and expansion of education of all levels has a strong negative effect on the income share of the top 20 percent population, suggesting that education, on the whole, might redistribute income from the top 20 percent population to the lower and middle income groups of the population.

Results of investigations on a selective few countries are also worth noting in this context. Based on an examination of data in a few countries, viz., the Netherlands, the USA, Mexico and Nigeria, Ritzen (1977) concluded that "investment in education jointly with investments in physical capital are an important instrument for the implementation of optimal income distribution cum economic growth policies" (p.239). The general tendency is that higher relative preferences for inequality minimization require higher levels of trained labor, jointly with higher physical capital stocks. However, from a theoretical model, recently Adelman and Levy (1984) reaffirmed more clearly their earlier argument. They argued that human resource intensive accumulation strategies are socially preferable to accumulation of physical capital as an important strategy for income redistribution and poverty eradication.

Richards and Leonor (1981) related changes in educational distribution with later changes in income distribution in a few Asian countries. The data on the distribution of educational assets and work incomes among the workers at two points of time in Sri Lanka and the Philippines indicate that the distribution of education and income appears to improve over time. However, they conclude that "overall distribution of work incomes probably owes much more to the distribution of occupations and to factors operating on occupational income independently of educational level, than to the distribution of education" (p.175).

From a sample of 30 countries, including 10 advanced and 20 less developed countries, Harbison (1977) examined the differential impact of formal and non-formal types of education on income distribution and found that both had a significant influence, but that formal schooling had a stronger effect on income differentials; and argued that it might be advantageous to curtail the public outlays for higher education and allocation of greater proportions to primary education would be appropriate. He also argued that non-formal education could have a more significant effect on income distribution than formal education.

The contribution of education to reduction in absolute poverty was also clearly recognized (Ribich 1968). For example, a lion's share of the funds of the 'war on poverty' in the US was allocated for education and training programs to build up human capital potential of the poor (see Schultz, 1966). But empirical investigations that analyzed quantitative relationships between education and poverty are indeed not many. An analysis of 66 less developed countries led Fields (1980b) to note clearly that "in each of the countries studied, the incidence of poverty decreases with educational attainment". Tilak (1986) also found for 29 countries on which data on poverty were available, significant negative correlation between education and poverty. The value of the regression coefficient of education on poverty declines by increasing levels of education, from literacy to higher level.

There are a few important micro studies also on the subject, besides studies on distributional aspects of public expenditure on education, that we refer to later. In the US according to the earlier works of Mincer (1958) schooling was the main cause of skewness in earnings distribution. Just over half of the inequality in earnings in US can be explained in terms of the inequality in educational attainment of workers (Mincer 1974 and 1976).

A study on Brazil (Langoni 1973a) showed that distribution of income became more unequal between 1960 and 1970 in part because the distribution of schooling became more unequal. The increase in variance in education of the labor force is found to be responsible for increase in income inequality. Educational differences explained 33 per cent of inequalities in the distribution of income during this period. University education in the country expanded much more rapidly than primary education. Obviously, the pattern of expansion of education (higher *versus* primary) and the distribution of earnings are highly related. In fact Langoni found that education was by far the most important one for explaining individual differences in income (see also Langoni 1973b). Velloso (1975) also argued the same: distribution of schooling is positively related to distribution of earnings in Brazil. Fishlow (1972) who also analyzed Brazilian evidence, also felt that varying the distribution of schooling in the labor force should have a direct effect on the distribution of earnings. Variance in the schooling of the labor force can be reduced directly concentrating on investment in lower levels of education.

Marin and Psacharopoulos (1976) found that an increase in the average level of schooling of the population not only is a socially profitable investment, but also "might not have the alleged bad side effect of worsening the size distribution of income" (p.337). In fact, as far as primary education is concerned, it has a significant effect on inequality in earnings. A 10 percent increase in enrollments would reduce the variance in (log) earnings by 4.7 percent in Mexico. Similarly, providing secondary school to 10 percent of those with primary school graduates in US would reduce the variance in earnings by 4.4 percent. Further, expansion of higher education by 5 percent would worsen inequality index by 2 percent. Similar evidence is available for UK as well. Blaug, Dougherty and Psacharopoulos (1982) found that raising of minimum school age in England by one year is likely to reduce income inequality in a future steady state by 12-15 percent. Earlier Blaug and Morris (1978) found a higher effect of raising the school learning age from 15 to 16. This was estimated to have reduced the variance of logarithm of earnings by as much as 24 percent. Knight and Sabot (1983) found that inequality in incomes is less in Tanzania and Kenya the greater the supply of educated labor.

A few studies did however, report either limited or insignificant or contradictory effects of education on income inequalities. Ram (forthcoming) in a cross-nation study on 27 countries, concluded that the mean education of the labor force has an infinitisimally small and statistically insignificant effect on the Gini coefficient of income inequality.[19] Nevertheless, the effect is significant in the case of the less developed countries. Psacharopoulos (1978) has shown that after

---

[19]/ The simple coefficient of correlation between the two is -0.36, and statistically significant at 10 percent level.

controlling for personal, occupational and related characteristics, dispersion in earnings declines in UK by increase in mean years of schooling. The effect might be small but significant. Studies on Peru (by Toledo: see Carnoy et al 1979) and Mexico (by Baskin; and Lobo; see Carnoy et al 1979) also reported similar evidence, but the effect of education is found to be small. Education in El Salvador contributes to equalization in earnings distribution to some extent in public sector, but not much in private sector. Summing up the evidence from Latin American countries, Carnoy et al (1979, p.98) concluded that while schooling apparently plays a very important role in determining individual earnings in Latin America, the distribution of education in the labor force is not very important in influencing earnings distribution." Woo (1982) found that the equalizing potential of education is not large in Singapore. So is it in Nicaragua (Behrman et al 1985). Muta (1987) has shown that equalizing educational distribution does not completely reduce the income inequalities between several socio-economic groups in Japan. The effect of education is quite small in Philippines (Rodgers 1978). Dasgupta (1979) found that while public education in India and also in Colombia contribute to equality, the negative effects of private education are so high that the overall effect of education may be negative. The public efforts are not adequate to counter-act the disequalizing forces inherent in the private education systems.

On the other hand, some have strongly argued totally the other way. For instance, Foster (1980, p.201) stated that "schools and universities of Sub-Saharan Africa are the most important contemporary mechanism of stratification and redistribution of the continent. As Simmons and Alexander (1980) argued expansion of education, particularly increase in education level "has served to increase rather than decrease income inequality." The evidence on Chile (Johnston 1973; and Uthoff 1981) suggests that the changes in the distribution of schooling had a negative effect on income distribution. Although distribution of schooling in Mexico has become more equal, income distribution has become more unequal (Carnoy et al 1979).

Perhaps, government's direct policies may be more important. But government policies on wages, employment etc., do have direct effect on education. Hence, it may be difficult to separate the effect of education from state involvement in other development policies on income distribution. The potential effect of education on income distribution is negated in a good number of cases by the factors prevailing in the economy outside the education system, particularly the occupational patterns, employment discrimination, wage structure, etc. For example, Knight and Sabot (1987) found that public sector pay policies are more important than education expansion in Tanzania; but in Kenya education does have a significant effect. As Carnoy et al (1979, p.98) summed up, "government incomes policy, affecting the reward to different levels of schooling, different work sectors, different types of occupations and different regions of the country may be a much more important factors in understanding changes in income distribution." Hence Rice (1981, p.333) concludes that "exclusive reliance on educational programs for influencing the distribution of earnings will not provide the optimal social benefits". Bhaduri (1978, p.13) also argues that "human capital approach cannot be considered to be a general explanation of income differences [and] any policy prescription for income equalization mainly through equalization of educational opportunities should be considered inadequate in most cases."

Table 9

INCIDENCE OF UNEMPLOYMENT AMONG HOUSEHOLDS WITH DIFFERENT LEVELS OF INCOME IN GREATER BOMBAY, INDIA (1971)

Household Income (Rs. per month)	Incidence of Unemployment			
	Male		Female	
	Crude	Standardized	Crude	Standardized
0 - 100	11.23	38.49	-	-
101 - 200	8.42	7.41	6.41	4.98
201 - 300	5.48	9.54	31.05	31.82
301 - 400	6.13	5.01	11.39	9.85
401 - 500	5.12	3.89	15.94	12.27
501 - 750	4.44	3.08	10.27	6.37
751 - 1000	3.00	1.82	2.88	2.77
1001 - 1500	3.90	5.19	3.55	5.60
1500 +	-	-	-	-
All	5.69	5.69	9.65	9.65

Source: Bhagawati (1973, p.31).

For Lesotho, Cobbe (1983) also feels the same. Jencks et al (1972) of course argued that a substantial connection does not exist between inequality in the distribution of schooling and distribution of income. According to Bowles (1972), social class and family origins are more important determinants of income inequalities. Chiswick and Mincer (1972) found positive but small effects of school inequality on income inequality, but unemployment was more important than level of education or its distribution in income distribution in the US. Thurow (1975) extended the argument further to state that if the distribution of job opportunities does not change, the overall income distribution may not change even if more people are educated. After all, it may be noted that unemployment itself is a declining function of income, as shown in Table 9 on India. Despite similar problems, the earnings differentials by race in New Zealand are predicted to decline by increasing levels of education (Brosnan 1984).

Before we sum up it may be added that when inequality was decomposed and the determinants of income were analyzed in 13 out of 14 studies on 10 countries, education turned out to be the most significant factor, and in the lone exception (Thailand), education was the second most important factor (see Fields 1980b, pp.116-20). Thus on the whole, education is found to be one of the most important variables effecting income distribution.

2.4 Public Subsidization of Education and Equity

Education in most societies is highly subsidized by the government. This subsidization in general, and in higher education in particular, is said to have been producing several perverse effects on income distribution, as the public subsidies for higher education largely accrue to high income groups resulting in deterioration in income distribution.

An examination of private and social rates of return to education indicates that in many countries the level of subsidization of higher education exceeds that in primary education. For example, in Africa the index of subsidization[20] is 157 in higher education compared to 92 in primary education (Psacharopoulos 1985).

Alternatively, even if we were to consider only public recurring cost and the fee paid by the students, the difference being public subsidy, we note that higher education is highly subsidized. Quite surprisingly in a few countries where primary and secondary education are not provided free, higher education is totally free. For example, in Kenya students at secondary level pay 44 percent of the recurring cost as fees, while higher education is provided free. In many countries subsidies as a proportion of unit costs of higher education exceed the subsidies at primary and secondary education, as shown in Table 10.

That distribution of enrollments particularly in higher education favors high income groups is well documented. In many developing countries education itself is a privilege of a few high income groups, and this skewness in the distribution of enrollments intensifies by increasing levels of education.

Anderson (1987) has documented in a recent work the uneven distribution of enrollments in a number of countries by various socio-economic characteristics, such as father's schooling, father's occupation,

---

[20] This subsidization index for a given level of education is defined as the percent by which the private rate of return exceeds the social rate.

Table 10
PUBLIC SUBSIDIZATION OF EDUCATION (Around 1980)

Region and Country	Subsidies as % of Unit Recurrent Cost		
	Primary	Secondary	Higher
EAST AFRICA			
Botswana	100.0	97.3	100.0
Burundi	100.0	95.7	100.0
Kenya	96.0	56.3	100.0
Lesotho	91.0	57.9	95.0
Malawi	63.0	37.0	99.0
Mauritius	100.0	100.0	100.0
Somalia	100.0	100.0	100.0
Sudan	-	-	100.0
Swaziland	93.0	93.7	-
Tanzania	100.0	100.0	100.0
Uganda	73.0	75.7	-
Zambia	97.0	88.4	-
Zimbabwe	100.0	95.0	-
WEST AFRICA			
Burkina Faso	87.0	100.0	100.0
Central African Republic	97.5	97.3	-
Guinea	100.0	100.0	100.0
Mauritania	100.0	100.0	100.0
Nigeria	70.0	61.0	87.6
Sierra Leone	98.5	79.7	-
Togo	83.0	95.0	-
ASIA			
India	98.0	81.5	71.9
Indonesia	100.0	92.0	87.0
Korea	96.3	58.8	76.6
Malaysia	95.0	95.0	94.2
Pakistan	98.8	98.2	97.9
Philippines	-	-	96.3
Thailand	100.0	87.5	93.1
Solomon Islands	100.0	75.0	100.0
Turkey	100.0	100.0	85.0
Yemen Arab. Rep.	100.0	100.0	-
LATIN AMERICA AND THE CARIBBEAN			
Bolivia	99.2	99.6	99.0
Brazil	-	-	95.0
Chile	98.4	99.1	75.0
Colombia	-	-	96.4
Costa Rica	99.7	99.5	92.0
Dominican Republic	100.0	100.0	99.0
Ecuador	100.0	100.0	98.0
Guatemala	-	-	100.0
Haiti	93.2	96.6	-
Honduras	100.0	90.4	90.0
Mexico	-	30.0	99.7
Paraguay	95.9	98.0	99.3
Uruguay	99.5	99.6	95.0

Note: Public subsidy is defined as public recurrent cost minus the fees as percentage proportion of public recurrent cost.

- Not available.

Source: Based on Psacharopoulos et al (1986, p.55).

social status, etc. The evidence on distribution of enrollment by income groups is difficult to get, but some strong empirical evidence does exist. In Chile (Santiago) Anderson (1987, p.268) found that 63 percent of the enrollment in higher education belonged to the top household income quintile, and the corresponding proportion for the bottom two quintiles is hardly 8.7 percent.

On India, Tilak and Varghese (1985) documented some such evidence relating to higher education, and concluded that "higher education is even now a favorite sector of the privileged groups of the society. This is more so in the case of professional education".[21] A clear and highly regressive pattern of distribution can be noted in higher education sector in Bombay. The enrollment for the lowest income groups (whose annual income was less than Rs.3,000), constitutes a bare 8.7 percent of the total enrollment in higher education.

Some available evidence on a sample of countries is summarized in Table 11. It is clear from a large number of studies[22] that the proportion of enrollments in higher education is positively related to the economic class. This unequal distribution along with unequal public subsidization of higher education is generally found to be inequitable. The unequal subsidization and its implications are highlighted by Mingat and Tan (1985) in a very impressive way. With the help of enrollments and unit costs, Mingat and Tan analyzed the distribution of education resources (Table 12).

21/ See also Blaug et al (1969), and Bhagawati (1973).

22/ A few IIEP studies conducted in the context of a research project on higher education and employment (see Sanyal 1987) however, shows a different pattern from sample surveys of students: relatively larger proportion of middle-income groups in higher education.

Table 11

DISTRIBUTION OF STUDENTS IN HIGHER EDUCATION (%), BY INCOME

Country (Source)	Household Income Classes			
	Bottom 25%	Second Quartile	Third Quartile	Top 25%
Chile (Santiago) (Anderson, 1987)	3.5	5.2	28.4	62.9
	Bottom 40%	3rd Quintile	4th Quintile	Top 20%
Colombia (Selowsky, 1979)	4.3	8.1	20.4	67.2
Malaysia (Selowsky, 1979)	9.0	18.0	18.0	48.0
	National Family Income Quintiles			
	Bottom 40%	3rd Quintile	4th Quintile	Top 20%
Japan (James and Benjamin, 1987)	17.6	11.6	24.6	45.9
US (California) (James and Benjamin, 1987)	23.0	17.8	22.4	37.2
	Household Income Classes			
	Bottom 40%	Middle 30%	Top 30%	
Indonesia (Meessok, 1984)	4.0	10.0	86.0	
	Annual Income Classes			
	<Rs.3000	Rs.3001-6000	Rs.6001-9000	>Rs.9000
India (Bombay) (Panchamukhi, 1977)	8.7	17.6	20.6	53.1
	Parental Income Classes			
	<Rs.7200	Rs.7201-30000	>Rs.30000	
Pakistan (Husain et al., 1987)	18.9	57.0	24.1	

Table 12

DISTRIBUTION OF RESOURCES FOR EDUCATION (Around 1980)

	Primary		Higher Education	
	Population (%)	Resources (%)	Population (%)	Resources (%)
Africa				
Anglophone	83	39.0	1.2	26.4
Francophone	86	15.7	2.4	39.5
Asia				
South Asia	81	23.2	4.4	39.0
East Asia and Pacific	57	19.3	9.1	39.6
Latin America	56	16.3	12.0	42.1
Middle East and North Africa	64	18.8	9.4	44.9
Developing Countries	71	22.1	6.4	38.6
Developed Countries	20	8.3	21.0	36.7

Source: Mingat and Tan (1985, p.305).

In developing countries, 71 percent of those with primary or less education share only 22.1 percent of the resources, whereas 6.4 percent of those with higher education get 38.6 percent of these resources. The distribution is more skewed in Francophone Africa. They have also shown that with reallocation of resources, the coefficient of distribution of education resources can be substantially improved in all the regions of the world.[23]

Thus the pattern of allocation and financing of education may significantly influence the effect of education on income distribution. As Tullock (1983, pp.183-84) stated, "higher education is a highly regressive scheme for transferring funds from the people who are less well off to those who are well off." In a pioneering empirical study on this aspect, Hansen and Weisbrod (1969) analyzed the taxes and subsidies for higher education in California and concluded that the net effect was transfer of income from poor tax payers to the rich through public subsidization of higher education. Fields (1975) analyzed the distributional impact of public subsidization of higher education in a developing country, viz., Kenya. By an examination of the distribution of benefits, tax costs and tax payers by income class, Fields found that low-income students are under represented in higher education, and pay a larger share of the direct costs of education than their respective fraction of benefits, while the middle income families receive larger benefits and pay less. Thus, higher education seems to be redistributing resources from the poor to the middle income groups. However, Fields argues that it is not just the higher education that is inequitable, it is built into the whole education system. The cause for the inequity in higher education lies in the advance selection at the primary and secondary levels.

---

[23]/ See also Mingat and Tan (1986) for related additional evidence.

In another important study, Jallade (1974) analyzed the impact of public expenditure on education on income distribution in Colombia, and concluded that public financing of primary education actually redistributes income from the 13 percent richer families to 87 percent poorer families; the redistributive effect is particularly beneficial for the lowest 40 percent families. In the case of secondary education, the main beneficiaries are middle income groups, secondary education was found to be distributing income from both the 40 percent poorest and the 13 percent richest families to the middle income group.

But a study on Brazil (Jallade 1977; also 1982), where changes in the overall level of education are related to changes in the distribution of income, produced different conclusions that "education investment as such cannot reduce existing income inequality," as increased level of education has not led to narrowing of income differentials. The principal reason for this were inequality in access to education among different groups of population and inequality in employment opportunities. Even though education subsidies and taxes on lifetime earnings favor lower income groups, these two factors, viz., educational inequalities and employment opportunities offset the total effect of education on income distribution.

In an important study on the distribution of public expenditure in Malaysia, Meerman (1979) found a strong relationship between household income and enrollments in schools. Enrollments are an increasing function of income. It is only at primary level that a negative relationship between enrollments and income could be found, suggesting a progressive distribution of enrollments at primary level. But when the enrollments are adjusted for household size, and enrollment ratios (rates) are used, even at primary level, one finds a positive relationship. On the basis of public costs of education, Meerman further found that the distribution of public resources on education is quite uneven. While at every level of education it is the high income groups who benefit most, the disadvantage is less at primary level for low income groups.

Using a somewhat different approach, Bhagawati (1973) arrives at a similar conclusion: at all levels of education, richer classes receive greater benefits. Since at higher education, richer classes contribute a larger proportion of students, the benefits received by richer classes would be higher at higher levels of education. He argues:

> "For each class of education, the State (in capitalist LDCs) will subsidize the cost of education; the benefits of these subsidies will accrue disproportionately less to the poorer groups at each level of education; the higher the educational level being considered, the higher will be the average income level of the groups to which students belong; and the rate of governmental subsidization to higher education will be greater than that to primary education" (p.24).

Bhagawati explains these regressive effects of public subsidization with the help of differences in opportunity costs of education and employment probabilities.

In a study similar to Meerman (1979), Selowsky (1979) finds a slightly different pattern in Colombia. Low income quintiles have a larger share of enrollment in primary schools, whereas the opposite is true in higher education. On the other hand, the distribution of enrollments in secondary education favors the middle income groups. Selowsky also found a similar pattern in the distribution of public education subsidies: the subsidies at primary education were skewed in favor of low income groups, and subsidies at higher education the rich-income quintiles. Distribution of secondary education subsidies also favors the lower-income groups. Selowsky himself compared his results with those of earlier studies (e.g., Jallade 1974; and Urrutia and Sandoval 1974); and these comparisons do reveal that over time there has been improvement in the distribution of education subsidies at all levels. For instance, in 1966 only 34 percent of the primary education subsidies were received by the bottom two quintiles, as compared to 59 percent in 1974. At the other end, higher education subsidies received by the top 20 percent households were reduced from 83 percent to 60 percent during the same period.

Dasgupta and Tilak (1983) made a similar attempt on Indian data, and arrived at conclusions more or less similar to that of Selowsky. Based on distribution of enrollments and of public subsidies, Dasgupta and Tilak concluded that financing of primary education in India seems on the whole to be egalitarian. Secondary education also benefits the lower-income quintiles; and higher education benefits are concentrated in middle (second quintile and above) and high-income groups. Public financing of higher education in rural areas is to a large extent clearly pro-rich.[24]

Meesook (1984) presents a similar pattern on Indonesia: the distribution of enrollments as well as public subsidies at primary and junior secondary levels clearly favoring the lowest 40 percent population, and those at senior secondary and higher education favoring the top 30 percent population, the distribution being alarmingly skewed at higher education in favor of the top 20 percent population.

---

[24]/ See also Maitra (1985) who found not only that inequality in India is higher in rural areas than in urban areas, but also that it has increased over the years.

A study on Chile (Casteneda 1984) also reveals that the distribution of education subsidies, while on the whole is equitable, that at primary education favors the bottom 40 percent and middle 40 percent populations, while more than 60 percent of the subsidies at higher education goes to the top 20 percent population. A comparative study of the distributive effects of public subsidies in various sectors in five Latin American countries (Petrei 1987) provides more recent evidence from Chile, which shows a similar pattern, with more benefits accruing to the middle income group.[25]

The evidences from Argentina, Costa Rica, Dominican Republic and Uruguay (Petrei 1987) also fall into the same pattern: the education subsidies received by low-income groups decline by increasing levels of education.

Analyzing the evidence from Malaysia, Bowman *et al* (1986, p.144) observe that there can be no doubt about the strong contemporary regressive effect of the higher education subsidies in relation to education and (hence also to household income). However, aggregated results provide different results, as if the subsidies are distributed not very unequally.

If one has to summarize all the available evidence, given in Table 13, the distribution of education subsidies, on the whole seems to be equitable. More than 40 percent of the education subsidies go to the bottom 40 percent population in all the countries, except in Dominican Republic where the bottom two quintiles receive only a quarter of the total education subsidies; and in all countries, more than one-third of the subsidies are received by the middle 40 percent population. If we analyze

---

[25]/ Both studies refer more or less to the same period.

Table 13

DISTRIBUTION OF EDUCATION SUBSIDIES BY INCOME GROUP

Country (Source)	Year	Level of Education	Shares of the Population		
			Bottom 40%	Middle 40%	Top 20%
Colombia (Selowsky, 1979)	1974	Primary	59	36	6
		Secondary	39	46	16
		University	6	35	60
		All levels	40	39	21
Malaysia (Meerman, 1979)	1974	Primary	50	40	9
		Secondary	38	43	18
		University	10	38	51
		All levels	41	41	18
Malaysia (Bowman et al., 1986)		Higher	30	35	35
India (Dasgupta and Tilak, 1983)	1978	Elementary	61	31	8
		Secondary	51	34	15
		Higher	33	49	18
		All levels	45	40	15
Argentina (Petrei, 1987)	1980	Basic	64	27	9
		Secondary	47	39	14
		Higher	17	45	38
		All levels	48	35	17
Costa Rica (Petrei, 1987)	1982	Basic	62	31	7
		Secondary	45	43	11
		Higher	17	41	42
		All levels	42	38	20
Dominican Republic (Petrei, 1987)	1980	Basic	31	48	21
		Secondary	22	46	32
		Higher	2	22	76
		All levels	24	43	33
Uruguay (Petrei, 1987)	1982	Basic	71	22	7
		Secondary	46	43	12
		Higher	14	52	34
		All levels	52	34	14
Chile (Petrei, 1987)	1982	Basic	65	30	5
		Secondary	49	42	10
		Higher	12	34	54
		All levels	48	34	18
				Mid 30%	Top 30%
Indonesia (Meesook, 1984)	1978	Primary	51	27	22
		Jr. Secondary	45	21	33
		Sr. Secondary	22	23	55
		University	7	10	83
		All levels	46	25	29

by levels of education, in all the countries, excepting Dominican Republic, distribution of primary education subsidies favors the poorest 40 percent population; three-fourths to four-fifths of the secondary education subsidies are shared by bottom 40 percent population and the middle 40 percent population (except Indonesia and Dominican Republic). But the distribution of higher education subsidies is largely skewed in favor of the top 20 percent population, with a few major exceptions. For example, in India probably because of relative democratization of higher education, the middle 40 percent population benefits most from higher education subsidies, followed by the bottom 40 percent population. In Argentina and Costa Rica, it is the middle 40 percent and top 20 percent population that capture a large chunk of the higher education subsidies. Thus, in general, the distribution of higher education benefits is clearly anti-poor, and to a large extent pro-rich. That in general, public financing of primary education transfers the resources from the rich to the poor, and higher education does the opposite is shown more clearly in Figure 2.

On the whole, public subsidization of education has equitable effects, as the redistributive effect of primary education subsidies cancels out the regressive effect of higher education subsidies to a great extent. Some of the anomalies in this process can be corrected either through reforming the mechanism of education subsidization or through progressive measures in labor market, particularly relating to wages, employment, taxes, etc. For example, even though the distribution of enrollments in secondary and university education in Japan is in favor of high income groups, the progressive tax policies facilitate education to work as mechanism of redistribution of income from the rich to the poor, with the middle class receiving a relatively small net benefit (James and

FIGURE 2

DISTRIBUTION OF PERSONAL INCOME AND EDUCATION SUBSIDIES

(Colombia)

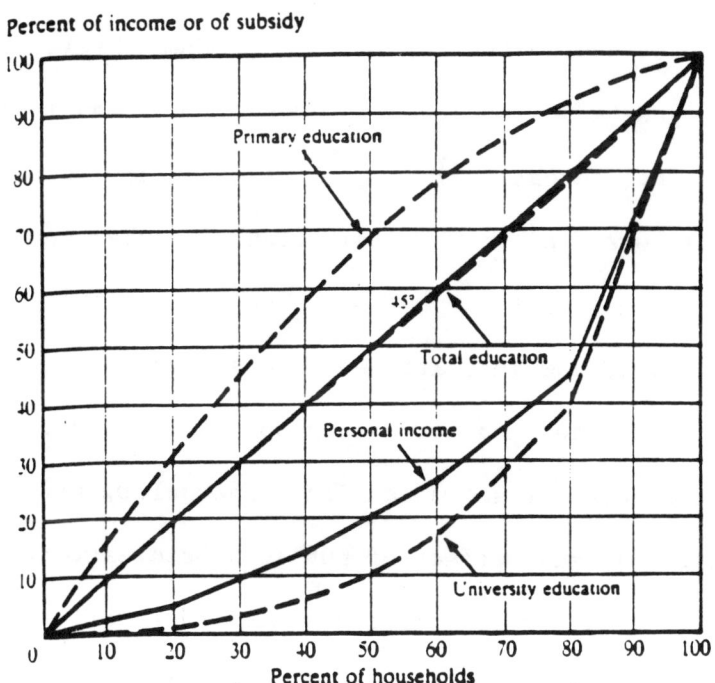

Source: Selowsky (1979, p.24).

Benjamin 1987). Comparing the general shares in payments and shares in enrollments of different income groups in public education, James and Benjamin find that public education (both high school and university levels) redistribute income from rich to the poor. Similarly in Europe, the pattern of higher education subsidies is found to be transferring the resources from the rich to the poor (Blaug and Woodhall 1979).

The perverse effects of public subsidization of higher education, particularly on inequality in education were analyzed by Psacharopoulos (1977b). He found through a cross section sample of 64 countries (42 less developed and 22 developed countries) that the higher the level of subsidization of higher education the higher the educational inequality. Further, he showed that educational inequality is higher in the less developed countries, where public subsidization of higher education is higher.

Rati Ram (1982) however, arrived at a somewhat different conclusion in a similar cross country study on the same problem. While noting that income inequality and educational inequality are related, Ram argued that the disequalizing effect of public subsidization of higher education is not statistically significant, and if there is any effect at all, it is stronger (but not significant) in the developed countries. In both developed and less developed countries, when separately analyzed, the relationship between subsidization at secondary or higher levels and income inequality is of course positive. However, he concluded that subsidy at the first level of schooling _appears_ to be an equalizer.

In an elaborate study of graduates of the University of Baroda in India, Shah and Srikantiah (1984) found that the general subsidization of 'any level' of education in general, and higher education in particular, is non-egalitarian having a much more pronounced stratified effect than the expected equalizer effect. They also found, however, that specific subsidies, i.e., scholarships, are an exception. Arguing that the present patterns of financing education in India have not accentuated inequalities, they however argue for concentrating on specific subsidies rather than on general subsidies in higher education. They also found that the lower the mean level of education, the higher the income inequalities and vice-versa.

The evidence from Cote d'Ivoire (Glewwe and de Tray 1988, p.27) on the specific subsidies, viz., scholarships, is quite striking. Even in absolute terms, the scholarships are extremely unevenly distributed. On average, the bottom 10 per cent population receive CFAF 156.3 per year per head as scholarships, while the corresponding figure is nearly 10 times higher (CFAF 1417.6) for the upper 70 percent population.

2.5 A Summary of the Earlier Evidence

In the preceding pages we have quickly surveyed the vast amount of research that is increasing at a rapid rate on education and economic growth, and on education and income distribution. On the former aspect, the studies covered included those that adopted a variety of methodologies, starting from (a) simple correlations, (b) residual methods, (c) production functions, (d) growth accounting equations, and (e) rates of return, besides historical narrations. With a very few exceptions, all the studies indicated positive contribution of education to economic growth. Then we also surveyed the literature on education and income distribution. The studies are of various types including (a) studies on correlation between mean education level and income inequality, (b) studies on correlation between distribution of education and distribution of income, (c) studies on correlation between changes in educational levels and changes in distribution of income inequalities within a country, and (d) studies on public subsidization of education and its effects on income distribution. In both the cases important cross-country and micro or country studies are reviewed.

To briefly summarize, the abundant research clearly establishes that:

- o education contributes to economic growth quite significantly, returns to education being fairly comparable with, if not more than, those to investment in physical capital;

- o the contribution of education is also significant in reducing poverty and improving income distribution, transferring sometimes resources from higher income groups to lower income groups;

- o both with respect to growth and income distribution, the contribution of primary education is more significant than that of higher levels of education;

- o even when we measure education's contribution in non-monetary terms, and measure in terms of physical productivity, say in agriculture, the positive and significant relationships hold good;

- o the contribution of education is higher in developing countries compared to developed countries; and

- o contribution is higher from investment in education of socio-economic weaker sections compared to investment in their respective counterparts.

What economists can measure, they measure; the rest is qualification. Scholars in economics of education could not quantify, but nevertheless take note of non-economic returns to education in reducing fertility, improving sanitation, improvement in performing household activities, making better citizens, improvement in quality of life, etc. Further, while research in economics of education does not refer to transformation of societies per se, the role of education in society's transformation is clearly recognized. After all, education, in its broad sense, is a great transformer. It influences the basic real constraints in development, that are related to social and economic dimensions and are structural in nature.

All this does not mean that all the research has been equivocal in supporting that education positively and significantly contributes to economic development, including growth and distribution. There are indeed important caveats. In some societies and at some stages of development, education and economic growth may not be related; and on a few occasions education may be a 'disequalizer.' In societies when only a small section of the people are educated, they will be able to command higher incomes as a result of scarcity. Further, if resources for education are limited, the limited resources may tend to be allocated unequally. Hence, if education expansion is to achieve the goal of greater equality, it must be pursued vigorously so that "the period of a transitional increase of inequality is made as brief as possible" (Sundrum 1987, p.221). On this aspect as a whole, Blaug (1981, p.85) has cautious optimism: "we have every reason to be cautious in predicting that a particular pattern of educational expansion throughout a poor country will necessarily alter the distribution of total income in that country in a particular direction; but that is not to say that the effect whatever it is, will be trivial or that all egalitarian aspirations of education reform can be dismissed as 'misguided liberalism'." He, however, added clearly: "it is possible to significantly equalize the distribution of income by specific policies designed to alter either the pattern of access to further schooling or the pattern of financing the existing numbers that achieve access" (p.80). Even the critics like Bowles (1978) and Carnoy admitted that "increased schooling may contribute significantly to economic growth and to more equitable distribution of earnings" (Carnoy et al 1982, p.64). However, all kinds of education expansion are not found to be desirable. Relatively it is the lower levels of education that pay most. In fact, subsidization of higher education is, in general, found to be highly regressive.

III. New Evidence

3. New Evidence

Now let us examine and analyze the latest available data on the problem with a different specification. Most earlier attempts used current enrollments to explain current levels of inequalities. But education may have a lagged effect, and not necessarily a concomitant effect. Accordingly we introduce time lag here in examining the relationship between education and poverty and inequality. This re-examination may help us to know what do the recent data suggest? Do they indicate the same relationships or any change in the nature and degree of relationships? We concentrate here on a few selected issues: (a) the effect of education on reducing poverty, (b) the effect of education on income shares of various groups of population classified by income classes, and (c) the effect of public subsidization of higher education on income inequality.

3.1 The Data

The sources of data we have relied on for the purpose on hand include three major categories: (i) the World Bank's published and unpublished data on poverty, income distribution, economic growth, etc.; (ii) the UNESCO's data on literacy and school enrollments mostly published in the <u>Statistical Yearbook</u>, and (iii) other sources, including Paukert (1973) for estimates of Gini coefficients of inequality, Fields (1988) for latest estimates of Gini coefficients and poverty, Psacharopoulos and Arriagada (1986) for estimates of schooling levels, etc. A few other minor sources are referred to later at appropriate places.

It is well known that such cross-country data are not perfect; they suffer from several inaccuracies, arising due to a variety of problems, differences in definitions, coverage, methods of conversion of GNP in local currencies into US dollars based on ordinary exchange rates,[26] methods of data collection, particularly on income distribution and poverty[27] etc., and as a result inter-country comparisons need to be made with caution. We cannot claim that the data used here are different and perfect; they also suffer from the same weaknesses. However, it may be added that these are the very data that are available to researchers, technocrats, policy makers and administrators around the world. Table A.1 in the Appendix gives a summary of the variables we use here, their definition, means and standard deviations.

3.2. Education and Poverty

Even though importance of education in reducing <u>absolute</u> poverty is clearly recognized, very few scholars examined empirically this relationship. Most scholars concentrated on examining the role of education in reducing <u>relative</u> income inequality. From the available evidence (e.g., World Bank 1980; Fields 1980c; and Tilak 1986), one expects

---

[26] See e.g., Azam and Guillaumont (1988) and Summers and Heston (1984).

[27] See e.g., van Ginnek and Jong-goo (1984). Almitir (1987) discussed on the reliability of income distribution estimates in Latin America. Fields (1988) has shown that of the available data on income distribution for 70 developing countries, only half the countries' data are somewhat comparable.

Table 14

Schooling and Poverty

	SCH		POVERTY		
	Year	SCH	Year	Rural	Urban
Mali	1976	0.5	1976	48	27
Pakistan	1975	1.2	1979	29	32
Morocco	1971	1.2	1979	45	28
Liberia	1974	1.3	1978	..	23
Haiti	1982	1.6	1977	78	55
India	1981	1.9	1979	51	40
Botswana	1971	2.0	1979	55	40
Honduras	1961	2.1	1978	55	14
Afghanistan	1979	2.1	1977	36	18
Rwanda	1978	2.2	1977	90	30
Tunisia	1975	2.2	1977	15	20
Cameroon	1976	2.2	1978	40	15
Bangladesh	1981	2.4	1977	86	86
Ethiopia	1978	2.6	1976	65	60
Malawi	1977	2.9	1977	85	25
Guatemala	1973	3.0	1980	74	66
Egypt, Arab Rep.	1976	3.3	1978	25	21
Kenya	1980	3.5	1978	55	10
Indonesia	1978	3.9	1980	44	26
Algeria	1977	4.0	1977	..	20
Yemen, Arab Rep.	1981	4.1	1978	20	..
Thailand	1974	4.1	1978	34	15
Paraguay	1972	4.3	1978	50	19
Lesotho	1976	4.3	1979	55	50
Nicaragua	1971	4.4	1978	19	21
Mauritius	1972	4.5	1979	12	12
Panama	1970	4.8	1978	30	21
Malaysia	1967	5.0	1980	38	13
Sudan	1974	5.5	1975	85	..
Zambia	1979	5.5	1978	..	25
Jordan	1975	5.6	1979	17	14
Costa Rica	1973	6.4	1977	..	34
Ecuador	1982	6.5	1980	65	40
Trinidad and Tobago	1980	6.6	1977	39	..
Bolivia	1970	6.9	1975	85	..
Jamaica	1978	6.9	1977	80	..
Peru	1981	7.0	1977	..	49
Philippines	1980	7.0	1980	41	32
Greece	1981	7.9	1970s	21	25
Korea, Rep. of	1980	8.0	1977	11	18

Note: SCH: Mean years of schooling of the labor force.
POVERTY: Percentage of people below poverty level.
.. Not Available.
Source: SCH: Psacharopoulos and Arriagada (1986);
POVERTY: BESD (Bank Economic and Social Data), World Bank, Washington, D. C.

that education and absolute poverty will be inversely related: the higher the level of education of the population, the lower would be the proportion of poor people in the total population, as education imparts knowledge and skills that are associated with higher wages. In addition to this direct effect of education, the effect of education on poverty could be indirect though its influence on fulfillment of basic needs like better utilization of health facilities, water and sanitation, shelter etc., (see e.g., Noor 1980), and on labor force participation, family size, etc., which in turn enhance the productivity of the people and yield higher wages and reduce inequality in earnings (see e.g., Blau et al 1988). While we do not propose to examine here these complicated indirect relationships, we wish to test a simple hypothesis that improvement in educational levels of the population would reduce the poverty ratio. Available data on poverty and mean years of schooling of the labor force (SCH)[28] are presented in Table 14. These figures on poverty compiled from the World Bank Data files (BESD: Bank's Economic and Social Data), refer to percent of population living below poverty level in the late 1970s. They are mostly available by rural and urban areas separately, but not for both areas together. Further, they are also available only for a few countries. The data show that there is a clear correlation between the proportion of poor people below the poverty level in rural/urban areas in a country and SCH. The

---

[28]/ Psacharopoulos and Arriagada (1986, p. 573) estimated mean years of schooling for 99 countries, using the following formula:

$$SCH = \{(LP1 \times YRSP/2) + (LP2 \times YRSP) + [LS1 \times (YRSP + YRSS/2)] + [LS2 \times (YRSP + YRSS)] + [LH \times (YRSP + YRSS + YRSH)]\} / 100$$

where
- SCH : mean number of years of schooling,
- LP1 : percentage of the labor force with incomplete primary schooling,
- YRSP: duration in years of primary education cycle,

Continued on next page

coefficient of correlation is -0.3430 in rural areas and -0.2165 in urban areas. Let us first analyze this relationship with the help of a simple equation of the following form:

$$POVERTY_j = f(ED_i) \qquad \ldots \qquad (Eqn.1)$$

where POVERTY refers to poverty ratio

[j = 1 (rural), and 2 (urban)]; and

ED_i to education variables.

The following five education variable are chosen:

LIT: Adult literacy rate (%)

SCH: Mean years of schooling of labor force,

ERP: Gross enrollment ratio at primary level (%)

ERS: Gross enrollment ratio at secondary level (%), and

ERH: Gross enrollment ratio at higher level (%).

Data on education variables are collected mostly from the UNESCO *Statistical Yearbook*(s).

Continued from previous page
- LP2 : percentage of the labor force with completed primary schooling,
- LS1 : percentage of the labor force with incomplete secondary schooling,
- YRSS: duration in years of secondary education cycle,
- LS2 : percentage of the labor force with completed secondary schooling,
- LH : percentage of the labor force with completed and incomplete higher education, and
- YRSH: duration in years of higher education cycle;

and it is assumed that the workers with incomplete primary and secondary education attended for half of the years of the corresponding level (e.g., if primary level = 6 years, LP1 = 3 years).

In most of the earlier attempts current levels of education are related to current levels of inequality.[29] It is more likely that education may have a lagged effect than a concomitant one (see Ram 1981). This will be true particularly with respect to school enrollment ratios. One can possibly hypothesize that enrollments in primary level of education may produce a significant effect only after 15-20 years, and those in secondary and higher education after about 5-10 years. On the other hand, literacy may have a lagged or an immediate effect on poverty and income distribution, and so is the case of SCH (mean years of schooling of labor force). Accordingly we introduce a time-lag in the educational variables and consider for the purpose on hand enrollments in primary education in 1965 (ERP65), enrollments in secondary and higher education in 1975 (ERS75 and ERH75), and literacy rates referring to 1975 (LIT75).

Equation 1 is estimated for rural and urban areas separately. We expect that in our model education will have a negative significant coefficient. The OLS estimates of Equation 1 based on these data are given here in Table 15 for rural and urban areas. As one expects high correlation between the five education variables, they are also alternatively tried in the equation. Mean years of schooling (SCH) is also an overlapping variable, covering all levels of education, and is perhaps one of the best measures of the available measures on educational development. This however, refers to the labor force only. This variable was tried alone in the equation given above.

29/ E.g., Adelman and Morris (1973); Ahluwalia (1974; 1976a; 1976b); Chenery and Syrquin (1975); Tilak (1986); and Psacharopoulos (1977a). That education variables are generally autocorrelated over time might be the basis for such a treatment by earlier scholars.

Table 15

EXPLAINING POVERTY: I

	R.1	R.2	R.3	R.4	R.5	R.6
Dependent Variable: $POVERTY_r$						
LIT75	-0.2783**					
	(2.355)					
ERP65		-0.3023***				-0.2362
		(3.159)				(1.469)
ERS75			-0.5028***			0.0368
			(3.511)			(0.109)
ERH75				-1.4351**		-0.7463
				(2.205)		(0.725)
SCH					-2.8792	
					(1.651)	
$\bar{R}^2$	0.0917	0.1473	0.1847	0.0969	0.0458	0.1306
F-Value	5.54	9.98	12.32	4.86	2.73	2.75
N	46	53	51	37	37	36
Dependent Variable: $POVERTY_u$						
LIT75	-0.1895*					
	(1.774)					
ERP65		-0.1728**				-0.1799
		(2.067)				(1.168)
ERS75			-0.1538			0.1063
			(1.121)			(0.285)
ERH75				-0.2247		0.0689
				(0.400)		(0.062)
SCH					-1.2399	
					(0.925)	
$\bar{R}^2$	0.0713	0.0867	0.0058	-0.0246	-0.0042	-0.0434
F-Value	3.15	4.27	1.26	0.16	0.85	0.53
N	43	47	45	36	36	35

Note: Constant term is included in the regression, but not presented here.
Figures in parantheses are t-values.
*** significant at 1% level   ** significant at 5% level.
* significant at 10% level.

But for SCH which is found, contrary to our expectations, to have no significant effect at all, all the education variables are found to be significant in explaining rural poverty; and all education variables, including SCH, have expected negative signs. Probably due to multicollinearity, when enrollments in all the three levels of education are regressed in a single equation (R.6), as already feared, no education coefficient turned out to be statistically significant. But when each education variable including literacy was regressed separately, all the coefficients are statistically significant, and have expected negative signs, indicating that education has a strong effect on reduction in poverty in rural areas. This is true for all levels of education, starting from rudimentary literacy to higher education.

However, contrary to the earlier results (Tilak 1986), according to which secondary education had the highest effect, followed by primary level, and literacy, and higher education has the least effect, we find here now the effect of education increasing by increasing levels of education, higher education having the highest effect, and mere literacy the least. We shall try to explain this deviation later.

Further, quite surprisingly, education is not strongly related to urban poverty. Even though most coefficients of education have expected negative signs, it is only in the case of literacy and primary level of education, we arrive at somewhat significant results, significant at 90 and 95 percent levels of confidence respectively. Thus it seems that education is more effective in reducing rural poverty than reducing poverty in urban areas; and even in urban areas it is the literacy and primary education that are relatively more important.

In modelling poverty, perhaps the most obvious variable is per capita income, and this is omitted in Equation 1. After all, poverty is also correlated with the level of economic development. The coefficient of correlation between poverty and GNP per capita is -0.4561 in rural areas and -0.3131 in urban areas. There seems to be a linear relationship between poverty and GNP per capita, meaning that economic growth automatically reduces poverty.[30] Hence it may be logical to include the income variable in Equation 1 in a linear form as follows:

$$POVERTY_j = \alpha + \beta_1 \, GNP/pc + \beta_2 \, EDi + \epsilon \quad \ldots \quad (Eqn.2)$$

where

GNP/pc refers to GNP per capita

and others are as defined earlier.

α, β_i, and ϵ are respectively the intercept term, the regression coefficients and the error term respectively.

The results are presented in Table 16. In the equations relating to rural areas, all the variables have expected signs, except ERS in R.6. Like in the earlier case SCH turned out to be statistically not significant. Literacy variable is also not found to be significant. It is only primary and higher education that turned to be significant, and when all the three

---

[30] A non-linear relationship of the kind that we use later in the case of explaining income distribution, is found in the present case to be not statistically significant. E.g., see the following estimated equation (with t-values in parentheses) for poverty in rural areas:

$$POVERTY_r = 204.61 - 33.997 \, lnGNP/pc + 1.506 \, [lnGNP/pc]^2$$
$$\quad\quad\quad\quad (1.68) \quad\quad (0.89) \quad\quad\quad\quad\quad (0.52)$$
$$\bar{R}^2: \; 0.308 \quad F\text{-Value } 10.00 \quad N = 48.$$

Table 16

EXPLAINING POVERTY: II

	R.1	R.2	R.3	R.4	R.5	R.6
Dependent Variable: POVERTY$_r$						
LIT75	-0.2134 (1.442)					
ERP65		-0.2117* (1.789)				-0.2833* (1.726)
ERS75			-0.3680 (1.607)			0.4301 (1.029)
ERH75				-1.1721* (1.735)		-1.4245 (1.262)
SCH					-0.0635 (0.026)	
GNP/pc	-0.0048 (1.215)	-0.0060* (1.703)	-0.0043 (1.073)	-0.0056* (1.864)	-0.0079* (1.852)	-0.0057 (1.426)
$\bar{R}^2$	0.1247	0.1812	0.1545	0.1685	0.0850	0.2064
F-Value	4.06	6.20	5.11	4.45	2.53	3.15
N	44	48	46	35	34	34
Dependent Variable: POVERTY$_u$						
LIT75	-0.1336 (1.029)					
ERP65		-0.1365 (1.192)				-0.1919 (1.224)
ERS75			0.1287 (0.576)			0.5706 (1.312)
ERH75				0.2685 (0.434)		-1.5748 (0.483)
SCH					0.3354 (0.178)	
GNP/pc	-0.0075 (1.511)	-0.0048 (1.107)	-0.0100* (1.927)	-0.0080* (1.938)	-0.0072 (1.497)	-0.0100* (1.823)
$\bar{R}^2$	0.1088	0.0990	0.0699	0.0565	0.0332	0.0620
F-Value	3.44	3.36	2.54	2.02	1.57	1.54
N	41	44	42	35	34	34

Note: Constant term is included in the regression, but not presented here.
Figures in parantheses are t-values.
* significant at 10% level.

enrollment variables are regressed along with GNP per capita, it is only primary education that turns out be significant. GNP per capita is also found to be not having any significant effect. The few variables that are significant are however, significant only at 10 percent level. In the urban areas again education is found to have no effect at all on poverty. Thus though on the whole the results from Equation 2 that includes GNP per capita are not better, the levels of significance and the magnitudes of the coefficients being lower, they do suggest that even after controlling for income variable, education may contribute towards reducing poverty. From the earlier results in Table 15 however, we do find more clearly that education has an independent effect on poverty in rural areas.

Now let us examine the recent data on the relationship between education and income distribution.

3.3 Education and Income Distribution

The level of economic development is generally found to be highly related to income inequality. Perhaps this is one of the most well researched areas.[31] GNP per capita when entered in the explanatory model in a quadratic form, one finds, in general, a U-shaped relationship between the income share of the bottom income group and economic development, or an inverted U-shaped relationship between income share of the high income group and GNP per capita, the regression coefficients of the two variables having opposite signs, contributing to the view that 'income distribution must get worse before it gets better'.[32] It is not only the variations in

---

[31]/ See e.g., Kuznets (1955, 1963); Paukert (1973); Chenery et al (1974); Chenery and Syrquin (1975); and Lecaillon et al (1984).

[32]/ See also Fields (1980c); and World Bank (1980, p.8).

the level of economic development, measured by logarithm of GNP per capita, but also the rate of growth in GNP per capita is generally found to be highly related to income distribution. Hence one has to take into account the rate of economic growth as well in any model that attempts at explaining income distribution. Accordingly, the influence of education on the variations in income shares of the population are attempted to be explained here by fitting the following equation[33] to the latest cross-country data:

$$SHARE_i = \alpha + \beta_1 [\ln GNP/pc] = \beta_2 [\ln GNP/pc]^2 + \beta_3 [GNP/pcGR] + \beta_4 [ED_i] + \epsilon_i \quad \ldots \text{(Eqn.3)}$$

where

$SHARE_i$ refers to income share of the population of the group i, i = 1, 2, and 3

i.e., $SHARE_1$ = income share of the bottom 40 percent population (BOT40)

$SHARE_2$ = income share of the middle 40 percent population (MID40)

$SHARE_3$ = income share of the top 20 percent or (top quintile) population (TOP20 or Q5)

GNP/pc: Gross National Product per capita

GNP/pcGR: Annual growth rate of GNP/pc, and

ED_i: Education variables.

---

[33] It may be noted that this is similar to most models used earlier. See for example, Ahluwalia (1974, p.27).

We expect in general, the regression coefficients of aggregate education variables, like LIT and SCH to be significant and positive in explaining $SHARE_1$ and $SHARE_2$, and to be negative and significant in case of $SHARE_3$, as education is believed to be a great equalizer. With respect to the three educational levels, given the earlier research evidence, one may expect the following: the regression coefficients of primary and secondary education to be positive and significant and that of higher education, that benefits the high income groups, to be negative in explaining $SHARE_1$ and $SHARE_2$, and exactly the opposite in explaining $SHARE_3$, i.e., higher education to have a positive effect on the income share of top quintile, and lower levels of education to have a negative effect, as expansion of mass education is not in the interests of the high income quintiles.

First, we estimated the above equation with SCH for ED_i. The results are very poor, the regression coefficients of SCH are statistically not significant, as we note in Table 17. Only the income variables turned out to be significant. That SCH and income variables are correlated may be a reason for the SCH to turn out to be statistically insignificant. As one expects, SCH and income shares are significantly correlated, the coefficients of correlation between SCH and $SHARE_i$ being 0.4343, 0.6728, and -0.5292 respectively for $SHARE_1$, $SHARE_2$, and $SHARE_3$. It is important to note that not only the SCH is positively correlated with $SHARE_1$ and $SHARE_2$, but also it is inversely correlated with the income share of the top income quintile, $SHARE_3$, and all the coefficients are fairly high. Hence, a simplified form of the above equation of the following form was fitted:

$$SHARE_i = f\ (\ GNP/pcGR,\ SCH\ ) \qquad \ldots \quad (Eqn.4)$$

Table 17

EXPLAINING INCOME SHARES: I

	BOT40	MID40	TOP20
lnGNP/pc	-16.6432***	-13.4727**	35.8797***
	(3.170)	(2.644)	(3.498)
lnGNP/pc^2	1.1648***	0.9978***	-2.5495***
	(3.345)	(2.964)	(3.748)
GNP/pcGR	0.4631	0.6713**	-1.6187***
	(1.612)	(2.046)	(3.046)
SCH	0.1020	0.3462	-0.3641
	(0.347)	(1.111)	(0.628)
$\bar{R}^2$	0.3047	0.5780	0.4711
F-Value	6.59	14.70	12.58
N	52	41	53

Note: Constant term is included in the regression, but not presented.
t-values are in parentheses.
*** significant at 1% level; ** significant at 5% level.

Equation 4 also of course, allows for controlling for the rate of economic growth. The estimates of this equation are presented in Table 18. The table also contains the results of yet another alternative specification, a simple equation in which only SCH is regressed on $SHARE_i$. Both yield closely similar results, as far as the regression coefficient of SCH and its level of significance are concerned.

It is clear that schooling, after controlling for rate of economic growth, contributes significantly to income distribution. As levels of schooling of the labor force rise, the income shares of both the bottom 40 percent population and middle 40 percent population rise. The middle 40 percent population however, benefit most. Nearly half the income shares of the middle 40 percent population could be explained by our equation. More importantly, the results also clearly confirm Kuznets' (1955) prediction that as the labor force gets more and more educated, income gets redistributed, from the top income quintile to the bottom 80 percent population.

Now that it is shown from the latest evidence that schooling has an independent effect towards improving income distribution, let us examine the evidence to see which level of education contributes most. This question is more important for educational policy makers. On the basis of earlier evidence we may expect lower levels of education to have positive effect on the income shares of the lower income groups and higher education a negative effect, and for top income quintile the converse may hold true.

The earlier model (Equation 3) using literacy and the enrollment ratios at different levels of education alternatively is estimated. The results for the three income groups are presented in Tables 19 through 21.

Table 18

EXPLAINING INCOME SHARES: II

	BOT 40		MID 40		TOP 20	
	R.1	R.2	R.1	R.2	R.1	R.2
GNP/pcGR		0.2709		0.4493		-1.3234**
		(0.893)		(1.274)		(2.268)
SCH	0.6288***	0.5862***	1.1414***	1.1135***	-1.7018***	-1.6212***
	(3.543)	(3.221)	(5.678)	(5.551)	(4.626)	(4.380)
$\bar{R}^2$	0.1736	0.1568	0.4386	0.4474	0.2670	0.3152
F-Value	12.55	5.74	32.25	17.19	21.40	12.97
N	56	52	41	41	57	53

Note: Constant term is included in the regression, but not presented.
t-values are in parentheses.
*** significant at 1% level; ** significant at 5% level.

First, we note clearly that, just as we found already in Table 17, as expected, here too lnGNP/pc and (lnGNP/pc)² have significant and opposite signs to each other in all the three sets of equations (excepting in Equations R.5 in which coefficients are not significant, though the signs are as expected), confirming the existence of a significant U-shaped relationship in the case of $SHARE_1$ and $SHARE_2$ (lnGNP/pc has a negative sign, and its squared variable a positive sign), and a significant inverted U-shaped relationship in the case of the income shares of the top income quintile (lnGNP/pc having a positive sign and the other a negative sign).

Secondly, the results also seem to conform to the general hypothesis of growth with equity, i.e, higher the rates of growth better the equity. According to our results, rate of growth (GNP/pcGR) and shares of TOP20 ($SHARE_3$) are significantly and inversely related. But the regression coefficients of the same variable are not significant in case of $SHARE_1$, even though the signs are positive; in case of $SHARE_2$, the results are mixed: only in two out of five equations (Table 20), viz., R.1 and R.4, the coefficients are statistically significant, but in all four cases, the sign is positive, suggesting that it is likely that higher rates of growth have only a positive effect on income distribution.

Now let us look at the results relating to education. The results are somewhat, but not drastically, different compared to earlier research. Let us note first the present results:

First, the income shares of the bottom 40 percent population is positively and significantly influenced by enrollments in secondary education, and less significantly influenced by literacy. Enrollments in higher education do not have anything to do with the income shares of the

Table 19

EXPLAINING THE INCOME SHARE OF THE BOTTOM 40% POPULATION

	R.1	R.2	R.3	R.4	R.5
lnGNP/pc	-17.7695***	-18.3860***	-15.5087***	-14.6461***	-7.1506
	(3.839)	(3.612)	(3.431)	(3.498)	(1.346)
lnGNP/pc^2	1.2000***	1.2856***	1.0234***	1.0299***	0.4338
	(4.051)	(3.932)	(3.317)	(3.707)	(1.193)
GNP/pcGR	0.3033	0.3572	0.3605	0.7579**	0.7986**
	(1.097)	(1.289)	(1.372)	(2.563)	(2.600)
LIT75	0.0560*				
	(1.747)				
ERP65		0.0237			-0.0755*
		(0.720)			(1.934)
ERS75			0.0849**		0.1398***
			(2.518)		(2.975)
ERH75				0.0222	0.0161
				(0.349)	(0.165)
$\bar{R}^2$	0.3403	0.3018	0.3665	0.3408	0.4162
F-Value	8.22	7.16	9.10	8.11	7.06
N	57	58	57	56	52

Note: Constant term is included in the regression, but not presented.
t-values in parentheses.
*** significant at 1% level; ** significant at 5% level.
* significant at 10% level.

Table 20

EXPLAINING THE INCOME SHARE OF THE MIDDLE 40% POPULATION

	R.1	R.2	R.3	R.4	R.5
lnGNP/pc	-15.3999***	-13.4642**	-10.0066**	-10.5328**	-2.3873
	(3.032)	(2.154)	(2.085)	(2.202)	(0.412)
lnGNP/pc^2	1.0775***	1.0277**	0.6850**	0.7998**	0.1469
	(3.400)	(2.600)	(2.142)	(2.567)	(0.379)
GNP/pcGR	0.3967*	0.4886	0.3875	0.6159*	0.4793
	(1.326)	(1.485)	(1.342)	(1.995)	(1.590)
LIT75	0.0830**				
	(2.064)				
ERP65		0.0172			-0.0706
		(0.385)			(1.543)
ERS75			0.1170***		0.1607***
			(3.507)		(3.584)
ERH75				0.0935	0.0507
				(1.528)	(0.564)
$\bar{R}^2$	0.5734	0.5025	0.5981	0.5472	0.6262
F-Value	15.45	11.86	16.63	14.29	12.17
N	44	44	43	45	41

Note: Constant term is included in the regression, but not presented.
t-values in parentheses.
*** Significant at 1% level; ** Significant at 5% level
* Significant at 10% level.

bottom 40 percent population: the regression coefficients are small and statistically insignificant (Table 19).

The middle 40 percent population also benefits in terms of their income share from secondary education, and literacy. The effect, as well as its statistical significance are of course higher in case of secondary education than literacy. The explanatory power of either equation is nearly 60 percent. The enrollments in primary and higher education are again not significantly related to the income shares of the middle 40 percent population.

Table 21 presents the estimated equations for the income share of the top 20 percent population. The results indicate that expansion of education of all levels, from literacy to higher level, has an adverse effect on the share of the top income quintile, secondary education having highest negative influence, followed by literacy and primary education. Higher education also has a negative, but not statistically significant effect. All this seems to indicate that education, whether it is literacy, primary, secondary or higher, has the potential of redistributing income from the top income quintile to the lowest 40 and middle 40 percent population.

We have noted earlier from the survey of previous research that primary education is probably a greater equalizer than other levels of education. Our present results do not indicate the same. They suggest that its place is taken over by secondary education. What could be the probable causes for this major difference in the results? It is difficult to explain. One can possibly hypothesize the following: With significant increases in educational levels of the population throughout the world, as discussed in Part I, it is quite possible that the threshold level of

Table 21

EXPLAINING THE INCOME SHARE OF THE TOP 20% POPULATION

	R.1	R.2	R.3	R.4	R.5
lnGNP/pc	36.2987***	42.2388***	29.7429***	27.5783***	20.0843*
	(4.106)	(4.288)	(3.405)	(3.509)	(1.951)
lnGNP/pc²	-2.4929***	-2.9497***	-1.9793***	-1.9747***	-1.2801*
	(4.411)	(4.664)	(3.316)	(3.784)	(1.816)
GNP/pcGR	-1.1950**	-1.2711**	-1.3373**	-2.1353***	-1.9580***
	(2.372)	(2.465)	(2.761)	(4.063)	(3.456)
LIT75	-0.1401**				
	(2.262)				
ERP75		-0.1201*			0.0483
		(1.861)			(0.634)
ERS75			-0.2094***		-0.2319**
			(3.190)		(2.529)
ERH75				-0.1484	-0.0780
				(1.228)	(0.411)
$\bar{R}^2$	0.4985	0.4625	0.5046	0.5288	0.6021
F-Value	15.17	13.48	15.51	16.71	11.60
N	58	59	58	57	53

Note: Constant term is included in the regression, but not presented.
t-values in parentheses.
*** significant at 1% level; ** significant at 5% level.
* significant at 10% level.

education for it to significantly and positively contribute to income distribution, changes to higher and higher levels of education, first from rudimentary literacy to primary, then from primary to secondary, and with more significant progress in educational level from secondary to tertiary level of education.[34] Further, with rapid progress in education, cross-country variance in the enrollment ratio at primary education might have declined, as many countries achieve near universalization,[35] and as such loses its (primary level's) significance in explaining the variations in income inequalities; and the contribution of secondary education may become more and more important, both in benefiting the bottom 40 percent population, and the middle 40 percent population, and in transferring resources away from the top income quintile, as we see here.

3.4 Public Subsidization of Higher Education and Income Inequality

Earlier scholars analyzed the distribution of public subsidies by income groups and found that the distribution has been uneven. A few scholars (Psacharopoulos 1977b; and Ram 1982) also examined the relationship between public subsidization of higher education and educational inequalities. The effect of public subsidization on income inequalities as such was not examined. Given the indications of earlier research, one can expect that public subsidization of higher education

---

[34] For example, the evidence from a developing country on the relationship between education and agricultural productivity is worth noting here. Data relating to India in early 1960s showed a strong relationship between primary education and agricultural productivity (Chaudhri 1968); but the data relating to the 1970s indicated that it was secondary education that was having more significant effect on labor productivity than primary education (Chaudhri 1979).

[35] For example, the coefficient of variation on enrollment ratio at primary level across the countries of the world declined from 0.4118 in 1965 to 0.2654 in 1984. (Based on Table A.1 in the Appendix.)

aggravates income inequality. We test this hypothesis here. Using Paukert (1973) data on Gini coefficients of income inequality, and the subsidization index in higher education (SUBSIDY)[36] given by Psacharopoulos (1977b), both referring to the period around 1970, an equation of the form

$$GINI = f(\ln GNP/pc, [\ln GNP/pc]^2, SUBSIDY) \quad \ldots \quad (Eqn. 6)$$

is estimated here on the data on 35 countries. Subsidy and the income inequality are positively correlated, the coefficient of correlation being 0.3818. Further, it is generally felt that the subsidy would be higher, the higher the GNP per capita. In fact, the evidence here indicates that the index of subsidization and GNP per capita are inversely related, the coefficient of correlation being -0.3948. In other words, it is in the low income countries, where the subsidy for higher education is higher.

The results of the regression equation are given in Table 22. From this it is clear that after controlling for the economic factors, the higher the level of subsidization of higher education, the higher the inequality in income. The regression coefficient of the SUBSIDY is small, but statistically significant (at 90 percent level of confidence). Further, when the same data are classified into higher income (GNP per capita above $1000) countries and low-income (GNP per capita below $1000) countries, we note that the results are statistically significant only in the case of the low income countries, and not in the developed countries. These estimated equations suggest that the general finding that subsidization of higher education accentuates income inequalities holds

---

[36]/ It is simply defined as the ratio of direct cost per student in higher education and the GNP per capita.

Table 22

HIGHER EDUCATION SUBSIDY AND INCOME INEQUALITY: REGRESSION ESTIMATES OF THE GINI

	All Countries	LDCs	DCs
lnGNP/pc	0.4352*** (3.201)	0.8204*** (3.073)	1.3549 (0.543)
lnGNP/pc^2	-0.0370*** (3.335)	-0.0727*** (3.005)	-0.0942 (0.563)
SUBSIDY	0.0043** (2.478)	0.0046** (2.619)	-0.0136 (0.272)
$\bar{R}^2$	0.3389	0.3173	-0.2480
F-Value	6.81	4.41	0.27
N	35	23	12

Note: LDCs are those with GNP per capita below $1000; and DCs are those with GNP per capita above $1000.
Figures in parantheses are t-values.
Constant term is included in the regression, but not presented.
*** significant at 1% level;   ** significant at 5% level
*   significant at 10% level.

good for low-income countries; but may not hold true for rich countries.[37] This is contrary to what Rati Ram (1982, p.46) concluded: "if there is such an effect [disequalizing effect of public support to higher education] at all, it appears to be stronger in the DCs than in the LDCs". Here we note that the inverse relationship between subsidization of higher education and income equality holds good in the poor countries and not in the rich countries.

3.5 A Short Summary

The fresh examination of the available data with improved specification that included lagged variables on education, as attempted here, provide some interesting insights into the complex relationships between education and income distribution. Most scholars earlier used current enrollment patterns to explain current levels of income inequalities, which gave scope for some skeptics (e.g., Ram 1981)[38] to express doubts on the role of education in improving income distribution. The improved specification here shows that there is no reason to cast such doubts. A few selective dimensions of the problem are examined here. They include, the role of education in reducing poverty, the relationship between education and income distribution, and public subsidization of higher education and inequality in incomes. The examination of various alternative hypotheses with the help of recent data and a slightly improved specification here reassert the role of education in reducing poverty, and in improving income distribution. The present evidence also

---

[37]/ The number of observations in the case of the sample of the developed countries is of course small, 12.

[38]/ See also Ram (forthcoming).

shows marginal deviations on the roles of relative levels of education from what the earlier research indicated. While primary education was found to have had a significant effect on income distribution earlier, now we find that it is the secondary level of education that has a more significant effect, and that primary education may not be adequate to produce any recognizable significant effect. Further, public subsidization of higher education increases not only educational inequalities as the earlier research shows, but also inequalities in income. A few more important details follow in the concluding section.

IV. Concluding Observations

The paper has a two-fold objective:

i) to present a survey of empirical evidence on the role of education in economic growth, poverty and income distribution; and

ii) to make a fresh examination of some aspects of the same problem with the help of a more acceptable specification and the latest available data.

The first objective is accomplished by making an extensive, but not necessarily an exhaustive, survey of the growing research in the area. The survey concentrated on (a) contribution of education to economic growth, (b) relationship between education and agricultural productivity, (c) contribution of education to improvement in income distribution and poverty, and (d) public subsidization of higher education and its proven effects on equity.

Discussion on methodology developments in the area was kept outside the framework of this paper; but the empirical survey did cover studies that had adopted a variety of methodologies, including historical narrative approaches, correlation analyses, regression equations, production functions, simultaneous equations, and rates of return. The survey also included cross-nation as well as micro level studies.

In the third part, a fresh empirical analysis is attempted on the relationship between education and poverty and income distribution, using the most recent data, and with a slightly improved specification, compared to earlier research. In the earlier research mostly current enrollment rates were used to explain current levels of income inequality. But critics argue that education may have a lagged effect, and as such current levels of inequality could be explained with the help of past educational situation, or current enrollments may explain only the future inequalities. Hence here we introduce time-lag in the educational variables, to find the effect of education. Using alternative measures of income distribution, *viz*., the Gini coefficient of income inequality, income shares of various population groups by income classes, and poverty ratio, we examined and found that the following hypotheses are true:

- As the literacy levels of the population and the enrollments in education increase, the proportion of population below the poverty level declines. This is true particularly with respect to rural poverty. Education may not have a significant effect on urban poverty.

- Education contributes positively and significantly to reduction in income inequality.

- It is the secondary education that has a more significant effect on the redistribution of income than primary education; higher education has, in general, either an insignificant or negative role in income distribution.

- The higher the level of public subsidization of higher education, the higher the income inequality. This is true in general, and also in the case of the less developed countries, but not in the case of the developed countries.

On the whole, looking at the education-income distribution relationships, and the explanatory power of the education variables, it is no surprise to argue that "no income distribution theory can claim to be complete without taking the dynamic nature of the human capital into full account" (Sahota 1978, p.14).

An important caveat of the present study may also be noted: education-development relationships are quite complex. The effect of education on poverty, equity and income distribution may be both direct and indirect in nature, as the net effect is contingent upon several other factors, including personal characteristics of the individuals, like the ability, the socio-economic home background, the labor market conditions -- the wage structure, employment/unemployment probabilities, tax structure, etc. Education may influence income distribution through influencing these and factors, like fertility, mortality, health that affect income distribution.[39] In the present paper we have ignored discussion on these factors, however important they are.

Secondly, education not only influences development, it itself is influenced by development. Particularly poverty and income inequalities are some of the important determinants of education development (see e.g., Bhagawati 1973; and Ram 1981 and 1985). Because of this two-way

---

39/ See Psacharopoulos and Woodhall (1985). Further, female labor force participation, which is also influenced by education, may reduce income inequality (see Winegarden 1987); population growth which is found to have been highly influenced by education is also found to be directly related to income inequality (see Morley 1981); and so on. If these indirect effects are taken into account, the total effect of education on income inequalties may be quite dominant, as Blau et al (1988) have shown. In fact, they found that the indirect effects have a "significant and dominant role."

relationship, the relative importance of the two simultaneous effects of education on development and of development on education are yet to be demonstrated satisfactorily (see Fields 1980a, p.276).

Despite these important limitations, the present evidence reconfirms some of the well-established theses on the role of education in improving income distribution, indicates a marginal departure as the relative roles of various levels of education, partly questions some of the doubts expressed by critics, e.g., on the role of public subsidization of higher education in the developing countries compared to the developed countries, and, in general, on the whole, reasserts that education is an important policy instrument that can be looked upon with hope towards improving income inequalities, and reducing poverty.

However, it may be claimed that all types of educational expansion may not necessarily produce desirable effects. With increasing levels of enrollment in primary education, a gradual shift may be made towards expansion of secondary education. Increasing allocation of resources for higher education at the cost of primary and secondary levels may produce not only an unbalanced education system, but also regressive effects on income distribution.

A large publicly-funded higher education may also have adverse effects on income distribution. There is every case for reduction in public subsidies for higher education and increase the fee levels. Instead of a steep general increase in fee levels, a discriminatory fee policy[40] based on income levels of the students' families may be highly progressive, besides generating additional non-public resources for higher education.

40/ See Tilak and Varghese (1985) for an elaboration of the argument. See also Rogers (1971); Jallade (1973); Fields (1975); Psacharopoulos (1977); and Armitage and Sabot (1985).

In the short run, education expansion may produce income inequalties within a society. Education planners should aim at shortening the 'period of transitional increase of inequality' to the extent possible.

Lastly, after all, education does not exist in vacuum. The positive effect of education on income distribution can be enhanced by complementary policies regarding taxation, employment, wage policies, etc.

REFERENCES

AERC: Agricultural Economics Research Centre (1971) *Primary Education in Rural India: Participation and Wastage*. Delhi: Tata McGraw-Hill.

Adelman, Irma (1975) "Development Economics - A Reassessment of Goals," *American Economic Review* 65 (2) May (Papers and Proceedings), pp.302-09.

Adelman, I., and A. Levy (1984) "The Equalizing Role of Human Resource Intensive Growth Strategies: A Theoretical Model," *Journal of Policy Modelling* 6 (2) July, pp.271-87.

Adelman I., and Cynthia T. Morris (1973) *Economic Growth and Social Equity in Developing Countries*. California: Stanford University Press.

Ahluwalia, Montek S. (1974) "Income Inequality: Some Dimensions of the Problem," in Chenery et al., pp.3-37.

Ahluwalia, M.S. (1976a) "Income Distribution and Development: Some Stylized Facts," *American Economic Review* 66 (2) May (Papers and Proceedings), pp.128-35.

Ahluwalia, M.S. (1976b) "Inequality, Poverty and Development," *Journal of Development Economics* 3, pp.307-42.

Altimir, Oscar (1987) "Income Distribution Statistics in Latin America and their Reliability," *Review of Income and Wealth* 33 (2) June, pp.111-56.

Anderson, C. Arnold (1987) "Social Selection in Education and Economic Development," EDT Series 82. Washington, D.C.: World Bank, Education and Training Department.

Armitage, J., and R.H. Sabot (1985) "Efficiency and Equity Implications of Subsidies of Secondary Education in Kenya," Research Memorandum No.99. Williamstown, Mass.: Williams College, Center for Development Economics (mimeo).

Arrow, Kenneth J. (1973) "Higher Education as a Filter," *Journal of Public Economics* 2 (3) July, pp.193-216.

Ashby, E. (1961) "On Universities and Scientific Revolutions," in A.H. Halsey, et al., eds., *Education, Economy and Society*. New York: Free Press.

Atkinson, Anthony B., ed., (1976) *The Personal Distribution of Incomes*. London: George Allen & Unwin.

Aukrust, O. (1959) "Investment and Economic Growth," reprinted in Bowman et al., eds., pp.190-204.

Azam, Jean-Paul and Sylviane Guillaumont (1988) "Methodological Problems in Cross-Country Analyses of Economic Growth," Policy, Planning, and Research Working Paper Series, WPS 22. Washington, D.C.: World Bank, International Economics Department.

Balassa, Bela (1965) "Public Finance and Social Policy -- Explanation of Trends and Development: The Case of Developing Countries," in Public Finance and Social Policy. Detroit, Michigan: Wayne State University Press, pp.41-58.

Balogh, Thomas, and P.Streeten (1963) "The Coefficient of Ignorance," reprinted in M. Blaug, ed., Economics of Education I, London: Penguin, 1968, pp.383-95.

Becker, Gary S. (1960) "Underinvestment in College Education," American Economic Review 50 (2) May (Papers and Proceedings), pp.346-54.

Becker, G.S. (1975) Human Capital. New York: Columbia University Press. [Second Edn.]

Becker, G.S., and B.R. Chiswick (1966) "Education and the Distribution of Earnings," American Economic Review 56 (2) May (Papers and Proceedings), pp.358-69.

Behrman, Jere R. (1987) "Schooling and Other Human Capital Investments: Can the Effects be Identified?" Economics of Education Review 6 (3), pp.301-05.

Behrman, J.R., Barbara L. Wolfe, and David M. Blau (1985) "Human Capital and Earnings Distribution in a Developing Country: the Case of Prerevolutionary Nicaragua," Economic Development and Cultural Change 34 (1) October, pp.1-29.

Benavot, Aaron (1985) Education and Economic Development in the Modern World. Ph.D. Dissertation, Stanford University (unpublished).

Benavot, A., and Phyllis Riddle (1988) "The Expansion of Primary Education, 1870-1940: Trends and Issues," Sociology of Education 61 (3) July, pp.191-210.

Bennett, W.S. Jr., (1967) "Educational Change and Economic Development," Sociology of Education Spring, pp.101-14.

Bhaduri, Amit (1978) "Education and the Distribution of Personal Income: An Analysis of Issues and Policies," Industry and Development (UNIDO), 2, pp.3-14.

Bhagwati, Jagdish (1973) "Education, Class Structure and Income Equality," World Development 1 (5) May, pp.21-36.

Blau, D.M., J.R. Behrman, and B.L. Wolfe (1988) "Schooling and Earnings Distributions with Endogenous Labour Force Participation, Marital Status and Family Size," *Economica* 55 (219) August, pp.297-316.

Blaug, Mark (1972) "The Correlation between Education and Earnings: What Does it Signify?" *Higher Education* 1 (1) February, pp.53-76. [Reprinted in Blaug (1987), pp.76-99.]

Blaug, M. (1976) "The Empirical Status of Human Capital Theory: A Slightly Jaundiced Survey," *Journal of Economic Literature* 14 (3) September, pp.827-55. [Reprinted in Blaug (1987), pp.100-28.]

Blaug, M. (1981) "Thoughts on the Distribution of Schooling and the Distribution of Earnings in Developing Countries," in *Planning Education for Reducing Inequalities*. Paris: UNESCO:IIEP, pp.77-93.

Blaug, M. (1982) "The Distributional Effects of Higher Education Subsidies," *Economics of Education Review* 2 (3) Summer, pp.209-31. [Reprinted in Blaug (1987), pp.204-26.]

Blaug, M. (1987) *The Economics of Education and the Education of an Economist*. Hampshire, England: Edward Elgar.

Blaug, M., and J. Morris (1978) "The Distribution of Schooling and the Distribution of Earnings: Some British Evidence," (mimeo).

Blaug, M., and M. Woodhall (1979) "Patterns of Subsidies to Higher Education in Europe," *Higher Education* September, pp.31-63. [Reprinted in Blaug (1987), pp.166-96.]

Blaug, M., C.R.S. Dougherty, and G. Psacharopoulos (1982) "The Distribution of Schooling and the Distribution of Earnings: Raising the School Leaving Age in 1972," *The Manchester School of Economics and Social Studies*, 50 (1) March, pp.24-40.

Blaug, M., P.R.G. Layard, and M. Woodhall (1969) *The Causes of Graduate Unemployment in India*. London: Allen Lane the Penguin.

Bowles, Samuel (1971) "Class Power and Mass Education," Harvard University, mimeo.

Bowles, S. (1972) "Schooling and Inequality from Generation to Generation," *Journal of Political Economy* 80 (3) Part II: Supplement, May/June, pp.S219-51.

Bowles, S. (1978) "Capitalist Development and Educational Structure," *World Development* 6 (6) June, pp.783-96.

Bowman, Mary J. (1966) "The Human Investment Revolution in Economic Thought," *Sociology of Education* 39 (2) Spring, pp.111-37.

Bowman, M.J. (1980) "Education and Economic Growth: An Overview," in King, ed., pp.1-71.

Bowman, M.J., and C.A. Anderson (1963) "Concerning the Role of Education in Development," in C. Geertz, ed., *Old Societies and New States*. Glencoe, Illinois: Free Press, pp.249-79.

Bowman, M.J., B. Millot, and E. Schiefelbein (1986) "An Adult Life Cycle Perspective on Public Subsidies to Higher Education in Three Countries," *Economics of Education Review* 5 (2), pp.135-45.

Bowman, M.J., M. Debeauvais, V. Komarov, and J. Vaizey, eds., (1968) *Readings in the Economics of Education*. Paris: UNESCO.

Brosnan, P. (1984) "Age, Education and Maori Pakeha Income Differences," *New Zealand Economic Papers* 18, pp.49-62.

Carnoy, Martin, Jose Lobo, A. Toledo, and J. Velloso (1979) *Can Educational Policy Equalize Income Distribution?* Westmead, England: Saxon House for the International Labour Organization.

Carnoy, M., H. Levin, R. Nugent, S. Sumra, C. Torres, and J. Unsicker (1982) "The Political Economy of Financing Education in Developing Countries," in IDRC, pp.39-86.

Casteñeda, T. (1984) "La Evolución del Gasto Social en Chile y su Impacto Redistributivo," Dept. of Economics, University of Chile [cited in Psacharopoulos, et al., 1986].

Chaudhri, D.P. (1968) *Education and Agricultural Productivity in India*. Ph.D. Thesis (unpublished). Delhi: University of Delhi.

Chaudhri, D.P. (1979) *Education, Innovations and Agricultural Development*. London: Croom Helm for the International Labor Organization.

Chenery, Hollis B., and M. Syrquin (1975) *Patterns of Development 1950-1970*. New York: Oxford for the World Bank.

Chenery, H.B., M.S. Ahluwalia, C.L.G. Bell, J.H. Duloy and R. Jolly (1974) *Redistribution with Growth*. London: Oxford for the World Bank.

Chiswick, Barry R. (1971) "Earnings, Inequality and Economic Development," *Quarterly Journal of Economics* 85 (1) February, pp.21-39.

Chiswick, B.R. (1974) *Income Inequality: Regional Analysis within a Human Capital Framework*. New York: National Bureau of Economic Research.

Chiswick, B.R., and C. U. Chiswick (1987) "Income Distribution and Education," in Psacharopoulos, ed., pp.255-61.

Chiswick, B.R., and J. Mincer (1972) "Time-series Changes in Personal Income in the United States from 1939 with Projections to 1985", *Journal of Political Economy* 80 (2) Part II: Supplement, May-June, pp.S34-S66.

Chiswick, Carmel U. (1982) "Education and Labor Markets in LDCs," in Lascelles Anderson and Douglas M. Windham, eds., *Education and*

Development: Issues in the Analysis and Planning of Post-Colonial Societies. Lexington: Lexington Books, pp.99-112.

Cobbe, J.H. (1983) "The Educational System, Wage and Salary Structure, and Income Distribution: Lesotho as a Case Study," Journal of Developing Areas 17 (2) January, pp.227-42.

Cochrane, Susan H., D.J. O'Hara, and J. Leslie (1980) "The Effects of Education on Health," Staff Working Paper No. 405., Washington, D.C.: World Bank.

Colclough, Chrisopher (1982) "The Impact of Primary Schooling on Economic Development: A Review of Evidence," World Development 10 (3) March, pp.167-85.

Correa, Hector (1964) "Quality of Education and Socio-Economic Development," Comparative Education Review June, pp.11-17.

Curle, Adam (1964) "Education, Politics and Development," Comparative Education Review February, pp.226-45.

Dasgupta, Ajit K., and Jandhyala B.G. Tilak (1983) "Distribution of Education among Income Groups: An Empirical Analysis", Economic and Political Weekly 18 (33) August 13, pp.1442-47.

Dasgupta, Asim K. (1979) "Income Distribution, Education and Capital Accumulation." (670-19) Washington, D.C.: World Bank, (mimeo).

Dean, Edwin, ed., (1984) Education and Economic Productivity. Cambridge: Ballinger.

Denison, E.F. (1962) Sources of Economic Growth in the United States and the Alternatives Before us. Supplementary Paper No. 13. New York: Committee for Economic Development.

Denison, E.F. (1979) Accounting for Slower Economic Growth. Washington, D.C.: The Brookings.

Easterlin, R.A. (1961) "Israel's Development: Past Accomplishments and Future Problems," Quarterly Journal of Economics 75 (1) February, pp.63-86.

Easterlin, R.A. (1981) "Why Isn't the Whole World Developed?" Journal of Economic History 41 (1), pp.1-19.

Emi, K. (1968) "Economic Development and Educational Investment in the Meiji Era," in Bowman, et al., eds., pp.94-106.

Fields, Gary S. (1975) "Higher Education and Income Distribution in a Less Developed Country," Oxford Economic Papers 27 (2) July, pp.245-59.

Fields, G.S. (1980a) "Education and Income Distribution in Developing Countries: A Review of Literature", in King, ed., pp.231-315.

Fields, G.S. (1980b) <u>Poverty, Inequality and Development</u>. Cambridge: Cambridge University Press.

Fields, G.S. (1980c) "Assessing Progress toward Greater Equality of Income Distribution," in William P. McGreevey, ed., <u>Third World Poverty: New Strategies for Measuring Development Progress</u>. Lexington, Mass.: Lexington Books, pp.47-81.

Fields, G.S. (1987) "Measuring Inequality Change in an Economy with Income Growth," <u>Journal of Development Economics</u> 26 (2) August, pp.357-74.

Fields, G.S. (1988) "Poverty, Inequality and Economic Growth" (RPO 673-73), Washington D.C.: World Bank (mimeo).

Fishlow, A. (1972) "Brazilian Size Distribution of Income," <u>American Economic Review</u> 62 (2) May (Papers and Proceedings), pp.391-402.

Fishlow, A. (1975) "Income Distribution and Human Capital: Some Further Results for Brazil," in M. Parkin and A.R. Nobay, eds., <u>Contemporary Issues in Economics</u>. Manchester: Manchester University Press, pp.354-79.

Foster, Phillip (1977) "Education and Social Stratification in Less Developed Countries," <u>Comparative Education Review</u> 21 (2 & 3) June-October, pp.258-69.

Foster, P. (1987) "The Contribution of Education to Development," in Psacharopoulos, ed., pp.93-100.

Foxley, Alejandro (1979) <u>Redistributive Effects of Government Programmes: the Chilean Case</u>. Oxford: Pergamon for the International Labour Organization.

Freeman, Richard (1976) <u>The Overeducated American</u>. New York: Academic.

Fuller, Bruce, K. Gorman, and J. Edwards (1984) "The Influence of School Investment Quality on Economic Growth: An Historical Look at Mexico," pp.32-74 in S. Heyneman, and D. S. White, eds., <u>The Quality of Education in Developing Countries</u>. Washington, D.C.: The World Bank, pp.32-74.

Glewwe, Paul and D. de Tray (1988) "The Poor During Adjustment: A Case Study of Cote d'Ivoire," LSMS Working Paper No.47. Washington, D.C.: The World Bank.

Graham, J.W., and W.W. McMahon (1987) "Personal Earnings Variation and Education," in Psacharopoulos, ed., pp.261-66.

Grand, Julian L. (1982) "The Distribution of Public Expenditure on Education," <u>Economica</u> 49 (193) February, pp.63-68.

Griliches, Zvi (1964) "Research Expenditures, Education, and the Aggregate Agricultural Production Function," <u>American Economic Review</u> 54 (6) December, pp.961-74.

Griliches, Z. (1970) "Notes on the Role of Education in Production Functions and Growth Accounting," in W. Lee Hansen, ed., Education, Income and Human Capital, New York: Columbia University Press, pp.71-114.

Griliches, Z., and Dale W. Jorgenson (1966) "Sources of Measured Productivity Change: Capital Input," American Economic Review 61 (2) May (Papers and Proceedings), pp.50-61.

Hansen, W. Lee, and Burton A. Weisbrod (1969) "The Distribution of Costs and Direct Benefits of Public Higher Education: The Case of California," Journal of Human Resources 4 (2) Spring, pp.176-91.

Harbison, F.H. (1973) Human Resources and the Wealth of Nations, New York: Oxford.

Harbison, F.H. (1977) "The Education-Income Connection," in C.R. Frank and R. C. Webb, eds., Income Distribution and Growth in the Less-Developed Countries. Washington, D.C.: Brookings, pp.127-58.

Harbison, F.H., and C.A. Myers (1964) Education, Manpower and Economic Growth. New York: McGraw-Hill.

Haveman, Robert H., and Barbara L. Wolfe (1984) "Education, Productivity and Well Being," in Dean, ed., pp.19-55.

Hayami, Yujiro and Vernon W. Ruttan (1970) "Agricultural Productivity Differences among Countries," American Economic Review 60 (5) December, pp.895-911.

Hicks, Norman (1980) "Economic Growth and Human Resources." Staff Working Paper No. 408, Washington D.C.: World Bank.

Hines, F., L. Tweeten, and M. Redfern (1970) "Social and Private Rates of Return to Investment in Schooling by Race-Sex Groups and Regions," Journal of Human Resources 5 (3) Summer, pp.318-40.

Horn, R. and A-M. Arriagada (1986) "The Educational Attainment of the World's Population: Three Decades of Progress," EDT Discussion Paper No. 37. Washington, D.C.: World Bank.

Husain, T., Bikas C. Sanyal, Mohammad Hashim Abbasi and Shahrukh Rafi Khan (1987) Higher Education and Employment Opportunities in Pakistan. Research Report No. 60. Paris: International Institute for Educational Planning.

IDRC: International Development Research Centre (1982) Financing Educational Development. Ottawa.

Jain, Shail (1975) Size Distribution of Income: A Compilation of Data. Washington, D.C.: World Bank.

Jallade, Jean-Pierre (1973) "Financing of Education: An Examination of Basic Issues," Staff Working Paper No.157. Washington D.C.: The World Bank.

Jallade, J-P. (1974) *Public Expenditures on Education and Income Distribution in Colombia*. World Bank Occasional Paper No. 18. Baltimore: John Hopkins for the World Bank.

Jallade, J-P. (1977) "Basic Education and Income Inequality in Brazil: The Long-Term View," Staff Working Paper No. 268. Washington, D.C.: World Bank.

Jallade, J-P. (1982) "Basic Education and Income Inequality in Brazil," *World Development* 10 (3) March, pp.187-97.

James, Estelle and Gail Benjamin (1987) "Educational Distribution and Income Redistribution through Education in Japan," *Journal of Human Resources* 22 (4) Fall, pp.469-89.

Jamison, Dean T., and Lawrence J. Lau (1982) *Farmer Education and Farm Efficiency*. Baltimore: John Hopkins for the World Bank.

Jencks, Christopher, M. Smith, H. Acland, M.J. Bane, D. Cohen, H. Gintis, B. Heyns and S. Michelson (1972) *Inequality: A Reassessment of the Effect of Family and Schooling in America*. New York: Basic Books.

Jimenez, Emmanuel (1986) "Public Subsidization of Education and Health in Developing Countries: A Review of Equity and Efficiency," *World Bank Research Observer* 1 (1) January, pp.111-29.

Johnston, C.E. (1973) *Educación y Distribución del Ingreso*. Santiago, Chile: University of Chile (Thesis paper). [Cited in Carnoy et al (1982)].

Jorgenson, Dale W. (1984) "The Contribution of Education to US Economic Growth: 1948-73," in Dean, ed., pp.95-162.

Kahan, A. (1963) "Some Russian Economists on Returns to Schooling and Experience," in Bowman et al., eds., pp.399-410.

Kanamori, H. (1972) "What Accounts for Japan's High Rate of Growth?" *Review of Income and Wealth* 18 (2) June, pp.155-172.

Kendrick, J.W. (1977) *Understanding Productivity: An Introduction to the Dynamics of Productivity Change*. Baltimore: John Hopkins.

Kendrick, J.W. (1981) "International Comparisons of Recent Productivity Trends," in W. Fellner, ed., *Essays in Contemporary Economic Problems: Demand, Productivity and Population*. Washington, D.C.: American Enterprise Institute for Public Policy Research, pp.125-70.

King, Timothy, ed., (1980) "Education and Income," Staff Working Paper No. 402. Washington, D.C.: World Bank.

Knight, J.B., and R.H. Sabot (1983) "Educational Expansion and the Kuznets Effect," *American Economic Review* 73 (5) December, pp.1132-36.

Knight, J.B., and R.H. Sabot (1987) "Educational Expansion, Government Policy and Wage Compression," Journal of Development Economics 26 (2) August, pp.201-21.

Komarov, V. (1968) "The Relationship Between Economic development and the Development of Education," in Bowman et al., eds., pp.85-92.

Kothari, V.N. (1970) "Disparities in Relative Earnings among Different Countries," Economic Journal 80 (319) September, pp.605-16.

Krueger, Anne O. (1968) "Factor Endowments and Per Capita Income Differences among Countries," Economic Journal 78 (311), September, pp.641-59.

Kuznets, Simon (1955) "Economic Growth and Income Inequality," American Economic Review 45 (1) March, pp.1-28.

Kuznets, S. (1963) "Quantitative Aspects of Economic Growth of Nations III: Distribution of Income by Size," Economic Development and Cultural Change 11 (2) Part II, January, pp.1-80.

Langoni, Carlos G. (1973a) "A Distribucao da Penda e Desenvolvimento Economico do Brasil," Rio de Janerio: Editora Expressao e Cultura. [cited in Carnoy et al (1982)].

Langoni, C. G. (1973b) "Income Distribution and Economic Development in Brazil," Conjuntura Econmica 27 (9) Septembro. [Reprint, Rio de Janerio: BNH Information Office].

Lecaillon, Jacques, Felix Paukert, Christian Morrisson, and Dimitry Germidis (1984) Income Distribution and Economic Development: An Analytical Survey. Geneva: International Labour Office.

Lee, Kiong-Hock and George Psacharopoulos (1979) "International Comparisons of Educational and Economic Indicators: Revisited," World Development 7 (11 & 12) November-December, pp.995-1004.

Leipziger, D.M. (1981) "Policy Issues and the Basic Human Needs Approach," in D.M. Leipziger, ed., Basic Needs and Development. Cambridge, Mass.: Oelgeschtager, Gunn & Hain Publishers, pp.107-36.

Leipziger, D.M. and M. Lewis (1980) "Social Indicators, Growth and Distribution," World Development 8 (4) April, pp.299-302.

Lewin, Henry (1984) "Assessing the Equalization Potential of Education," Comparative Education Review 28 (1) February, pp.11-27.

Lewin, K., J.A. Little, and C. Colclough (1932) "Adjusting to the 1980's: Taking Stock of Educational Expenditure," in IDRC., pp.13-38.

Liu, P.W., and Y.C. Wong (1981) "Human Capital and Inequality in Singapore," Economic Development and Cultural Change 29 (2) January, pp.275-93.

Lockheed, Marlaine E., Dean T. Jamison and Lawrence J. Lau (1980) "Farmer Education and Farm Efficiency: A Survey," *Economic Development and Cultural Change* 29 (1), October, pp.37-76.

Lucas, R.E.B. (1977) "Is there a Human Capital Approach to Income Inequality," *Journal of Human Resources* 12 (3) Summer, pp.387-95.

Lundgreen, P. (1976) "Educational Expansion and Economic Growth in Nineteenth-Century Germany," in L. Stone, ed., *Schooling and Society: Studies in the History of Education*. Baltimore: John Hopkins, pp.20-66.

McClelland, D. (1966) "Does Education Accelerates Economic Growth?", *Economic Development and Cultural Change* 14 (3) April, pp.257-78.

McMahon, Walter W. (1984) "The Relation of Education and R&D to Productivity Growth," *Economics of Education Review* 3 (4), pp.299-313.

McMahon, W.W. (1987a) "Consumption and Other Benefits of Education," in Psacharopoulos, ed., pp.129-33.

McMahon, W.W. (1987b) "Externalities in Education" in Psacharopoulos, ed., pp.133-37.

Maitra, Tares (1985) *Public Services in India: An Analysis of Their Consumption in West Bengal*. Delhi: Mittal.

Marin, Alan and George Psacharopoulos (1976) "Schooling and Income Distribution," *Review of Economics and Statistics* 58 (3) August, pp.332-38.

Marris, Robin (1982) "Economic Growth in Cross Section: Experiments with Real Product Data, Social Indicators, Model Selection Procedures, and Policy Benefit/Cost Analysis", Discussion Paper. London: University of London, Birbeck, Department of Economics.

Meerman, J. (1979) *Public Expenditure in Malaysia: Who Benefits and Why?* New York: Oxford for the World Bank.

Meesook, Oey A. (1984) "Financing and Equity in the Social Sectors in Indonesia." Staff Working Paper No. 703. Washington, D.C.: World Bank.

Meyer, J., M. Hannan, R. Rubinson and G. Thomas (1979) "National Economic Development 1950-1970: Social and Political Factors," in J. Meyer and M. Hannan, eds., *National Development and the World System*. Chicago: University of Chicago Press, pp.85-116.

Mincer, Jacob (1958) "Investment in Human Capital and Personal Income Distribution," *Journal of Political Economy* 66 (4) August, pp.281-302.

Mincer, J. (1970) "The Distribution of Labor Incomes: A Survey with Special Reference to Human Capital Approach," *Journal of Economic Literature* 8 (1) March, pp.1-26.

Mincer, J. (1974) <u>Schooling, Experience and Earnings</u>. Cambridge, Mass.: National Bureau of Economic Research.

Mincer, J. (1976) "Progress in Human Capital Analysis of the Distribution of Earnings," in Atkinson, ed., pp.136-92.

Mingat, Alain and Jee-Peng Tan (1985) "On Equity in Education Again: An International Comparison," <u>Journal of Human Resources</u> 20 (2) Spring, pp.298-308.

Mingat, A., and J-P.Tan (1986) "Who Profits from the Public Funding of Education: A Comparison of World Regions," <u>Comparative Education Review</u> 30 (2) May, pp.260-70.

Morley, Samuel A. (1981) "The Effect of Changes in Population on Several Measures of Income Distribution," <u>American Economic Review</u> 71 (3) June, pp.285-94.

Muta, Hiromitsu (1987) "Equalization Potential of Education in Income Distribution in Japan," Rio de Janerio: Sixth World Congress of Comparative Education, (mimeo).

Noor, Abdun (1980) "Education and Basic Needs," Staff Working Paper No.450. Washington D.C.: The World Bank.

Panchamukhi, P.R. (1977) "Fee Financing of Education in India," in <u>Studies in Economics of Education and Fiscal Economics Vol. II. 1974-1977</u>. Bombay: Research Unit in Economics of Education, Department of Economics, University of Bombay (mimeo).

Patel, Surendra J. (1985) "Educational 'Miracle' in Third World, 1950 to 1981," <u>Economic and Political Weekly</u> 20 (31) August 3, pp.1312-17.

Paukert, Felix (1973) "Income Distribution at Different Levels of Development: A Survey of Evidence," <u>International Labour Review</u> 108 (2 & 3) August-September, pp.97-125.

Peasle, Alexander (1965) "Elementary Education as a Pre-requisite for Economic Growth," <u>International Development Review</u> 7, pp.19-24.

Peasle, A.L. (1967) "Primary School Enrollments and Economic Growth," <u>Comparative Education Review</u> 11 (1) February, pp.57-68.

Peasle, A.L. (1969) "Education's Role in Development," <u>Economic Development and Cultural Change</u> 17 (3) April, pp.293-318.

Petrei, A.H. (1987) <u>El Gasto Público Social y sus Efectos Distributivos</u>. Rio de Janeiro: Programa de Estudios Conjuntos sobre Integración Económica Latinoamericana.

Psacharopoulos, George (1973) <u>Returns to Education: An International Comparison</u>. Amsterdam: Elsevier.

Psacharopoulos, G. (1977a) "Unequal Access to Education and Income Distribution," <u>De Economist</u> 125 (3) September, pp.383-92.

Psacharopoulos, G. (1977b) "The Perverse Effects of Public Subsidization of Education or How Equitable is Free Education?" <u>Comparative Education Review</u> 21 (1) February, pp.69-90.

Psacharopoulos, G. (1978) "Labor Market and Income Distribution: The Case of the U.K.," in Wilhelm Krelle and Anthony F. Shorrocks, eds., <u>Personal Income Distribution</u>. Amsterdam: North-Holland, pp.421-40.

Psacharopoulos, G. (1981) "Education, Employment and Inequality in LDC's," <u>World Development</u> 9 (1) January, pp.37-54.

Psacharopoulos, G. (1982) "Education and Society: Old Myths versus New Facts," in Lord Roll of Ipsden, ed., <u>The Mixed Economy</u>. London: Macmillan, pp.145-61.

Psacharopoulos, G. (1984) "Contribution of Education to Economic Growth: International Comparisons," in J.W. Kendrick, ed., <u>International Comparisons of Productivity and Causes of the Slowdown</u>. Cambridge: American Enterprise Institute/ Ballinger, pp.335-60.

Psacharopoulos, G. (1985) "Returns to Education: A Further International Update and Implications," <u>Journal of Human Resources</u> 20 (4) Fall, pp.584-604.

Psacharopoulos, G., and A-M. Arriagada (1986) "The Educational Attainment of the Labour Force: An International Comparison," <u>International Labour Review</u> 125 (5) September-October, pp.561-74.

Psacharopoulos, G., and M. Woodhall (1985) <u>Education for Development</u>. New York: Oxford for the World Bank.

Psacharopoulos, G., J-P Tan and E. Jimenez (1986) <u>Financing Education in Developing Countries: An Exploration of Policy Options</u>. Washington, D.C.: World Bank.

Psacharopoulos, G., ed., (1987) <u>Economics of Education: Research and Studies</u>. Oxford: Pergamon.

Rado, E.R., and R. Jolly (1965) "The Demand for Manpower: An East African Case Study," <u>Journal of Development Studies</u> 1 (3) April, pp.226-51.

Ram, Rati (1981) "Inequalities in Income and Schooling: A Different Point of View," <u>De Economist</u> 129 (2), pp.253-61.

Ram, R. (1982) "Public Subsidization of Schooling and Inequality of Educational Access: A New World Cross Section Study," <u>Comparative Education Review</u> 26 (1) February, pp.36-47.

Ram, R. (1984) "Population Increase, Economic Growth, Educational Inequality and Income Distribution: Some Recent Evidence," <u>Journal of Development Economics</u> 14 (13) April, pp.419-28.

Ram, R. (1985) "The Role of Real Income Level and Income Distribution in Fulfillment of Basic Needs," <u>World Development</u> 13 (5) May, pp.589-94.

Ram, R. (1987) "International Evidence on the Relation Between Educational Expansion and Schooling Inequality in the Labor Force," Normal, Ill.: Illinois State University, Department of Economics (mimeo).

Ram, R. (forthcoming) "Can Educational Expansion Reduce Income Inequality in Less Developed Countries?" Economics of Education Review.

Razin, Assaf (1977) "Economic Growth and Education: New Evidence," Economic Development and Cultural Change 25 (2) January, pp.317-324.

Ribich, T. (1968) Education and Poverty. Washington, D.C.: Brookings.

Rice, R. (1981) "Can Educational Policy Affect the Distribution of Earnings?: A Quantitative Exploration," Journal of Policy Modelling 3 (3) October, pp.317-35.

Richards, P. and M. Leonor (1981) Education and Income Distribution in Asia. London: Croom Helm for the International Labour Organization.

Ritzen, J.M.M. (1977) Education, Economic Growth and Income Distribution. Amsterdam: North-Holland.

Rodgers, G.B. (1978) "An Analysis of Education, Employment, and Income Distribution Using an Economic-Demographic Model of the Philippines," Population and Employment Working Paper. Geneva: International Labour Office.

Rogers, Daniel (1971) "Financing Higher Education in Less Developed Countries," Comparative Education Review 15 (1) February, pp.20-27.

Rosen, Shervin (1976) "Human Capital: A Survey of Empirical Research," in R. Elthrenberg, ed., Research in Labor Economics. Greenwich: Johnson, pp.3-39.

Sahota, Gian S. (1978) "Theories of Personal Income Distribution: A Survey," Journal of Economic Literature 16 (1) March, pp.1-55.

Sanyal, Bikas C. (1987) Higher Education and Employment: An International Comparative Analysis. London: Falmer.

Schultz, T. Paul (1987) "Education Investments and Returns in Economic Development," Center Discussion Paper No.528, Yale Station: Yale University, Economic Growth Center.

Schultz, Theodore W. (1961a) "Investment in Human Capital," American Economic Review 51 (1) March, pp.1-17.

Schultz, T.W. (1961b) "Education and Economic Growth," in N.B. Henry, ed., Social Forces Influencing American Education. Chicago: National Society for Study of Education, pp.46-88.

Schultz, T.W. (1963) Economic Value of Education. New York: Columbia University Press.

Schultz, T.W. (1966) "Investment in Poor People," Seminar on Manpower Policy and Programs. Washington, D.C.: Department of Labor, Office of Manpower Policy Evaluation Research.

Schultz, T.W. (1975) "The Value of the Ability to Deal with Disequilibria," Journal of Economic Literature 13 (3) September, pp.827-46.

Selowsky, Marcelo (1969) "On the Measurement of Education's Contribution to Growth," Quarterly Journal of Economics 83 (3) August, pp.449-63.

Selowsky, M. (1979) Who Benefits from Government Expenditures? A Case Study of Colombia. New York: Oxford for the World Bank.

Shah, K.R. and S. Srikantiah (1984) Education, Earnings and Income Distribution: An Inquiry into Equity Issues involved in the Government Financing of Higher Education in India: A Study of the M S University of Baroda. New Delhi: Criterion.

Shortlidge, Richard L. Jr. (1973) "A Socioeconomic Model of School Attendance in Rural India," Ithaca: Cornell University, Department of Agricultural Economics (mimeo).

Simmons, John and L. Alexander (1980) "Factors which Promote School Achievement in Developing Countries: A Review of the Research," in J. Simmons, ed., The Education Dilemma. New York: Pergamon for the World Bank, pp.77-95.

Singer, Hans W. (1983) "The Role of Human Capital in Development," Pakistan Journal of Applied Economics 2 (1) Summer, pp.1-11.

Smith, Adam (1976) Wealth of Nations. New York: Modern Library, 1937.

Solow, Robert M. (1957) "Technical Change and the Aggregate Production Function," Review of Economics and Statistics 39 (3) August, pp.312-20.

Spence, A. Michael (1973) "Job Market Signaling," Quarterly Journal of Economics 87 (3) August, pp.355-74.

Strumilin, S.G. (1925) "The Economic Significance of National Education," reprinted in E.A.G. Robinson and J. Vaizey, eds., The Economics of Education. London: Macmillan, 1966, pp.276-323.

Summers, Robert and Alan Heston (1984) "Improved International Comparisons of Real Product and its Composition," Review of Income and Wealth 30 (2), June, pp.207-62.

Sundrum, R.M. (1987) Growth and Income Distribution in India: Policy and Performance since Independence. New Delhi: Sage.

Svennilson, I. (1964) "Economic Growth and Technical Progress: An Essay in Sequence Analysis," in J. Vaizey, ed., The Residual Factor and Economic Growth. Paris: OECD, pp.103-31.

Tan, Edita A. (1982) "Income Distribution, Underdevelopment and the Labor Market," Discussion Paper No.8202. University of the Philippines, School of Economics.

Tanzi, Vito (1978) "Tributacion, Gastos Educacionales y Distribucion Del Ingreso", in M. Brodersohn and M.E. Sanjurjo, eds., *Financiamento de la Educacion en America Lantina*. Mexico: Fondo de Cultura Economica, pp.233-54.

Taubman, Paul (1976) "Personal Characteristics and the Distribution of Earnings", in Atkinson, ed., pp.193-226.

Thurow, Lester (1972) "Education and Economic Inequality," *Public Interest* 28, Summer, pp.66-81.

Thurow, L. (1975) *Generating Inequality*. New York: Basic Books.

Thurow, L. (1977) "Education and Economic Equality," in J. Karabel and A.H. Halsey, eds., *Power and Ideology in Education*. New York: Oxford, pp.325-35.

Tilak, Jandhyala B.G. (1986) "Education in an Unequal World," in *Educational Planning: A Long Term Perspective*. New Delhi: Concept Publishers for National Institute of Educational Planning and Administration, pp.27-50.

Tilak, J.B.G. (1987a) *Economics of Inequality in Education*. New Delhi: Sage Publications for Institute of Economic Growth.

Tilak, J.B.G. (1987b) "Economic Growth and Life Expectancy," Washington D.C.: World Bank, Population Health and Nutrition Division, Population and Human Resources Department (draft).

Tilak, J.B.G. (1988a) "Socio-Economic Correlates of Infant Mortality in India," Washington D.C.: World Bank (mimeo).

Tilak, J.B.G. (1988b) "Comparative Development Indicators," (RPO 673-73) Washington D.C.: World Bank.

Tilak, J.B.G., and N.V. Varghese (1985) "Discriminatory Pricing in Education," Occasional Paper No. 8. New Delhi: National Institute of Educational Planning and Administration.

Tinbergen, Jan (1970) "A Positive and a Normative Theory of Income Distribution," *Review of Income and Wealth* 16 (2) June, pp.221-34.

Tinbergen, J. (1975) *Income Distribution: Analysis and Policies*. Amsterdam: North-Holland.

Tinbergen, J. (1977) "Income Distribution: Second Thoughts," *De Economist* 125 (3), pp.315-39.

Tinbergen, J. (1980) "Two Approaches to Quantify the Concept of Equitable Income Distribution," *Kyklos* 33 (1), pp.3-15.

Tullock, Gordon (1983) *Economics of Income Distribution*. Boston: Kluwer-Nijhoff.

Urrutia, M. and C.E. de Sandoval (1974) "Política Fiscal y Distribución del Ingreso en Colombia", *Revista de la República*, July, [cited in Meerman (1979), p.71].

Uthoff, A. (1981) "Changes in Earnings, Inequality, and Labour Market Segmentation," Santiago, Chile: International Normative Labour Organization, PREALC, Monograph 21, August.

Vaizey, John (1962) *Economics of Education*. London: Faber and Faber.

van Ginnek, Wouter, and Park Jong-goo, eds., (1984) *Generating Internationally Comparable Income Distribution Estimates*. Geneva: International Labour Office.

Velloso, J. (1975) *Human Capital and Market Segmentation: An Analysis of the Distribution of Earnings in Brazil*. Ph.D. Thesis. Stanford, Calif.: Stanford University.

Walters, Pamela Barnhouse (1981) "Educational Change and National Economic Development," *Harvard Educational Review* 51 (1) February, pp.94-107.

Walters, P.B., and R. Rubinson (1983) "Educational Expansion and Economic Output in the United States 1890-1969: A Production Function Analysis," *American Sociological Review* 48, pp.480-93.

Welch, F. (1970) "Education in Production," *Journal of Political Economy* 78 (1) January/February, pp.32-59.

Wheeler, D. (1980) "Human Resource Development and Economic Growth in Developing Countries: A Simultaneous Model," Staff Working Paper No. 407. Washington, D.C.: World Bank.

Winegarden, C.R. (1979) "Schooling and Income Distribution: Evidence from International Data", *Economica* 46 (181) February, pp.83-87.

Winegarden, C.R. (1987) "Women's Labour Force Participation and the Distribution of Household Incomes: Evidence from Cross-National Data," *Economica* 54 (214) May, pp.223-36.

Wolfe, Barbara L., and Behrman, J.R. (1984) "Who is Schooled in Developing Countries? The Roles of Income, Parental Schooling, Sex, Residence and Family Size," *Economics of Education Review* 3 (3), pp.231-45.

Woo, Lous K. (1982) *Equalizing Education and Earnings among Ethnic and Socio economic Groups in Singapore*. Ph.D. Thesis, Stanford University.

World Bank (1980) *Poverty and Human Development*. Washington D.C. [Reprint from *World Development Report 1980*.]

Wulf, Luc De (1975) "Fiscal Incidence Studies in Developing Countries: Survey and Critique," *International Monetary Fund Staff Papers*, 22 (1) March, pp.61-131.

Appendix

Table A.1

MEANS AND STANDARD DEVIATIONS OF THE VARIABLES

Variable	Definition	Mean	Standard Deviation	Number of Observations
$POVERTY_r$	Poverty in rural areas (% of population below poverty line)	50.55	22.89	53
$POVERTY_u$	Poverty in urban areas (% of population below poverty line)	31.15	16.89	47
BOT40	Income share of the bottom 40% population (%)	15.22	4.28	66
MID40	Income share of the middle 40% population (%)	37.09	4.74	46
TOP20 (Q5)	Income share of the top 20% population (%)	48.98	9.37	67
GNP/pc	Gross National Product per capita, 1985 ($)	3192.94	4443.73	109
lnGNP/pc	Log GNP per capita	7.11	1.42	109
$lnGNP/pc^2$	Square of log of GNP per capita	52.61	20.97	109
LIT	Adult Literacy Rate, (%), mid 1980s	61.60	27.84	63
ERP	Enrollment Ratio at Primary Level (%), 1984	90.82	24.11	119
ERS	Enrollment Ratio at Secondary Level (%), 1984	47.56	29.83	119
ERH	Enrollment Ratio at Higher Level (%), 1984	13.49	11.85	113
SCH	Mean Years of Schooling of the Labor Force	5.82	3.17	88
LIT60	Adult Literacy Rate (%), 1960	42.57	31.80	102
ERP65	Enrollment Ratio at Primary Level (%), 1965	76.14	31.89	125
ERS65	Enrollment Ratio at Secondary Level (%), 1965	25.32	22.46	122
ERH65	Enrollment Ratio at Higher Level (%), 1965	7.48	6.91	86
LIT75	Adult Literacy Rate (%), 1975	62.38	31.30	101
ERP75	Enrollment Ratio at Primary Level (%), 1975	82.71	29.10	117
ERS75	Enrollment Ratio at Secondary Level (%), 1975	38.16	28.10	117
ERH75	Enrollment Ratio at Higher Level (%), 1975	11.04	10.13	97
PRRP	Private Rate of Return to Primary Education (%)	32.01	24.89	23
PRRS	Private Rate of Return to Secondary Education (%)	17.71	11.75	38
PRRH	Private Rate of Return to Higher Education (%)	19.75	11.03	39
GINI-1	Gini Coefficients of Inequity (Paukert)	0.44	0.09	36
GINI-2	Gini Coefficient of Inequality (Fields)	0.47	0.10	32
SUBSIDY	Psacharopoulos' Subsidy Index	4.71	8.50	36

Table A.2

COEFFICIENTS OF CORRELATION AMONG THE EDUCATION VARIABLES, 1984

	ERP	ERS	ERH	LIT	SCH
ERP	1.0000				
ERS	.5007	1.0000			
ERH	.3534	.6012	1.0000		
LIT	.6093	.7196	.5559	1.0000	
SCH	.3467	.6985	.5495	.7998	1.0000

Table A.3

COEFFICIENTS OF CORRELATION BETWEEN CURRENT AND LAGGED EDUCATION VARIABLES

	1960	1965	1975	1984

Enrollment in Primary Level (N = 108)

1960	1.0000			
1965	.9329	1.0000		
1975	.7993	.8788	1.0000	
1984	.7178	.8111	.8803	1.0000

Enrollment in Secondary Education (N=102)

1960	1.0000			
1965	.9807	1.0000		
1975	.9281	.9596	1.0000	
1984	.8735	.9169	.9541	1.0000

Enrollment in Higher Education (N=79)

1960	1.0000			
1965	.9675	1.0000		
1975	.9040	.9098	1.0000	
1984	.8181	.8055	.8767	1.0000

Literacy (N=52)

	1960	1975	1984
1960	1.0000		
1975	.9321	1.0000	
1984	.9452	.9444	1.0000

DISTRIBUTORS OF WORLD BANK PUBLICATIONS

ARGENTINA
Carlos Hirsch, SRL
Galeria Guemes
Florida 165, 4th Floor-Ofc. 453/465
1333 Buenos Aires

AUSTRALIA, PAPUA NEW GUINEA, FIJI, SOLOMON ISLANDS, VANUATU, AND WESTERN SAMOA
Info-Line
Overseas Document Delivery
Box 506, GPO
Sydney, NSW 2001

AUSTRIA
Gerold and Co.
A-1011 Wien
Graben 31

BAHRAIN
MEMRB Information Services
P.O. Box 2750
Manama Town 317

BANGLADESH
Micro Industries Development Assistance Society (MIDAS)
House 56, Road 7A
Dhanmondi R/Area
Dhaka 1209

BELGIUM
Publications des Nations Unies
Av. du Roi 202
1060 Brussels

BRAZIL
Publicacoes Tecnicas Internacionais Ltda.
Rua Peixoto Gomide, 209
01409 Sao Paulo, SP

CANADA
Le Diffuseur
C.P. 85, 1501 Ampere Street
Boucherville, Quebec
J4B 5E6

CHINA
China Financial & Economic Publishing House
8, Da Fo Si Dong Jie
Beijing

COLOMBIA
Enlace Ltda.
Carrera 6 No. 51-21
Bogota D.E.
Apartado Aereo 4430
Cali, Valle

COSTA RICA
Libreria Trejos
Calle 11-13
Av. Fernandez Guell
San Jose

COTE D'IVOIRE
Centre d'Edition et de Diffusion Africaines (CEDA)
04 B.P. 541
Abidjan 04 Plateau

CYPRUS
MEMRB Information Services
P.O. Box 2098
Nicosia

DENMARK
SamfundsLitteratur
Rosenoerns Alle 11
DK-1970 Frederiksberg C.

DOMINICAN REPUBLIC
Editora Taller, C. por A.
Restauracion
Apdo. postal 2190
Santo Domingo

EGYPT, ARAB REPUBLIC OF
Al Ahram
Al Galaa Street
Cairo

The Middle East Observer
8 Chawarbi Street
Cairo

EL SALVADOR
Fusades
Edifico La Centro Americana 6o. Piso
Apartado Postal 01-278
San Salvador 011

FINLAND
Akateeminen Kirjakauppa
P.O. Box 128
SF-00101
Helsinki 10

FRANCE
World Bank Publications
66, avenue d'Iena
75116 Paris

GERMANY, FEDERAL REPUBLIC OF
UNO-Verlag
Poppelsdorfer Allee 55
D-5300 Bonn 1

GREECE
KEME
24, Ippodamou Street
Athens-11635

GUATEMALA
Librerias Piedra Santa
Centro Cultural Piedra Santa
11 calle 6-50 zona 1
Guatemala City

HONG KONG, MACAO
Asia 2000 Ltd.
6 Fl., 146 Prince Edward Road, W,
Kowloon
Hong Kong

HUNGARY
Kultura
P.O. Box 139
1389 Budapest 62

INDIA
Allied Publishers Private Ltd.
751 Mount Road
Madras - 600 002

Branch offices:
15 J.N. Heredia Marg
Ballard Estate
Bombay - 400 038

13/14 Asaf Ali Road
New Delhi - 110 002

17 Chittaranjan Avenue
Calcutta - 700 072

Jayadeva Hostel Building
5th Main Road Gandhinagar
Bangalore - 560 009

3-5-1129 Kachiguda Cross Road
Hyderabad - 500 027

Prarthana Flats, 2nd Floor
Near Thakore Baug, Navrangpura
Ahmedabad - 380009

Patiala House
16-A Ashok Marg
Lucknow - 226 001

INDONESIA
Pt. Indira Limited
Jl. Sam Ratulangi 37
Jakarta Pusat
P.O. Box 181

IRELAND
TDC Publishers
12 North Frederick Street
Dublin 1

ISRAEL
The Jerusalem Post
The Jerusalem Post Building
P.O. Box 81
Romema Jerusalem 91000

ITALY
Licosa Commissionaria Sansoni SPA
Via Lamarmora 45
Casella Postale 552
50121 Florence

JAPAN
Eastern Book Service
37-3, Hongo 3-Chome, Bunkyo-ku 113
Tokyo

JORDAN
Jordan Center for Marketing Research
P.O. Box 3143
Jabal Amman

KENYA
Africa Book Service (E.A.) Ltd.
P.O. Box 45245
Nairobi

KOREA, REPUBLIC OF
Pan Korea Book Corporation
P.O. Box 101, Kwangwhamun
Seoul

KUWAIT
MEMRB
P.O. Box 5465

MALAYSIA
University of Malaya Cooperative Bookshop, Limited
P.O. Box 1127, Jalan Pantai Baru
Kuala Lumpur

MEXICO
INFOTEC
Apartado Postal 22-860
Col. PE/A Pobre
14060 Tlalpan, Mexico D.F.

MOROCCO
Societe d'Etudes Marketing Marocaine
2 Rue Moliere, Bd. d'Anfa
Casablanca

NETHERLANDS
InOr-Publikaties b.v.
P.O. Box 14
7240 BA Lochem

NEW ZEALAND
Hills Library and Information Service
Private Bag
New Market
Auckland

NIGERIA
University Press Limited
Three Crowns Building Jericho
Private Mail Bag 5095
Ibadan

NORWAY
Narvesen Information Center
Bertrand Narvesens vei 2
P.O. Box 6125
N-0602 Oslo 6

OMAN
MEMRB Information Services
P.O. Box 1613, Seeb Airport
Muscat

PAKISTAN
Mirza Book Agency
65, Shahrah-e-Quaid-e-Azam
P.O. Box No. 729
Lahore 3

PERU
Editorial Desarrollo SA
Apartado 3824
Lima

PHILIPPINES
National Book Store
701 Rizal Avenue
Metro Manila

POLAND
ORPAN
Palac Kultury i Nauki
00-001 Warszawa

PORTUGAL
Livraria Portugal
Rua Do Carmo 70-74
1200 Lisbon

SAUDI ARABIA, QATAR
Jarir Book Store
P.O. Box 3196
Riyadh 11471

SINGAPORE, TAIWAN, BURMA, BRUNEI
Information Publications
Private, Ltd.
02-06 1st Fl., Pei-Fu Industrial
Bldg., 24 New Industrial Road
Singapore

SOUTH AFRICA
Oxford University Press Southern Africa
P.O. Box 1141
Cape Town 8000

SPAIN
Mundi-Prensa Libros, S.A.
Castello 37
28001 Madrid

SRI LANKA AND THE MALDIVES
Lake House Bookshop
P.O. Box 244
100, Sir Chittampalam A. Gardiner Mawatha
Colombo 2

SWEDEN
Fritzes Fackboksforetaget
Regenngsgatan 12, Box 16356
S-103 27 Stockholm

SWITZERLAND
Librairie Payot
6, rue Grenus
Case postal 381
CH 1211 Geneva 11

TANZANIA
Oxford University Press
P.O. Box 5299
Dar es Salaam

THAILAND
Central Department Store
306 Silom Road
Bangkok

TRINIDAD & TOBAGO, ANTIGUA, BARBUDA, BARBADOS, DOMINICA, GRENADA, GUYANA, JAMAICA, MONTSERRAT, ST. KITTS AND NEVIS, ST. LUCIA, ST. VINCENT & GRENADINES
Systematics Studies Unit
55 Eastern Main Road
Curepe
Trinidad, West Indies

TURKEY
Haset Kitapevi, A.S.
Davutpasa Caddesi
Sergekale Sokak 115
Topkapi
Istanbul

UGANDA
Uganda Bookshop
P.O. Box 7145
Kampala

UNITED ARAB EMIRATES
MEMRB Gulf Co.
P.O. Box 6097
Sharjah

UNITED KINGDOM
Microinfo Ltd.
P.O. Box 3
Alton, Hampshire GU34 2PG
England

URUGUAY
Instituto Nacional del Libro
San Jose 1116
Montevideo

VENEZUELA
Libreria del Este
Aptdo. 60.337
Caracas 1060-A

YUGOSLAVIA
Jugoslovenska Knjiga
YU-11000 Belgrade Trg Republike

ZIMBABWE
Longman Zimbabwe
P.O. Box ST 125, Southerton
Harare

Prices and credit terms vary from country to country. Consult your local distributor before placing an order.